Your Vision Torch!

An Innovator's Prescription for Igniting Your Dreams & Harnessing Your Vision.

The Princess of Suburbia™ Brand
FUMI. STEPHANIE. HANCOCK,
BSN, M.A., Ph.D.
Bestselling Author

ISBN-10: 1492952370   ISBN-13: 978-1492952374

:

YOUR VISION TORCH!
An Innovator's Prescription for Igniting
Your Dreams & Harnessing You Vision

The Princess of Suburbia ™ Brand
FUMI .S. HANCOCK, RN, BSN, MA, Ph.D.
Bestselling Author

YOUR VISION TORCH!

An Innovator's Prescription for Igniting Your Dreams & Harnessing Your Vision

Princess Fumi Stephanie Hancock, RN, MA. Ph.D.
The Princess of Suburbia ™ Brand

BESTSELLING AUTHOR

SUBSCRIBE TO MY EMAIL:
fumi@worldoffumihancock.com
princessinsuburbia@gmail.com

WEBSITE: www.worldoffumihancock.com

SOCIAL MEDIA CONNECTIONS:
http://about.me/fumihancock
WATCH & SUBSCRIBE TO MY POPULAR TV SHOW, The Princess in Suburbia TV:
www.youtube.com/user/princessinsuburbia
www.theprincessinsuburbia.com

LISTEN & SUBSCRIBE TO MY RADIO SHOW,
On the Air with Princess in Suburbia:
www.blogtalkradio.com/ontheairwithprincessinsuburbia

CAMBIUM BREAK HOLDINGS PUBLICATIONS
223 Towncenter Pkwy, # 2071, Spring Hill TN, 37174, US
Printed in the United States of America 2013

Authentic leadership begins with exercising authentic character. Thank you for respecting the hard work of this author.

Disclaimer and Terns of Use: The Author and Publisher has tried to be as accurate and complete as possible in the creation of this book, notwithstanding the fact that she does not warrant or represent at any time that the contents within are accurate due to the rapidly changing nature of the internet. While all attempts have been made to verify information provided in this publication the Author and Publisher assumes no responsibility for errors, omissions, or contrary interpretation of the subject matter therein. Any perceived slights of specific persons, peoples, or organizations are unintentional. In practical advice books, like anything else in life, there are no guarantees. This book is not intended for use as a source for legal, business, accounting or financial advice. All readers are advised to seek the services of competent professionals in the legal, business, accounting and finance field.

DEDICATION

To my husband, David Hancock, my wonderful children, Bola Thompson, Demola Thompson, my step daughters, Holly & Marlee, and my extended family, the Adumori Royal Family from Emure Kingdom in Ekiti State, Nigeria, my royal father, King Emmanuel Adebayo and Queen Adebayo, my parents, Prince Ademola & Princess Remi Ogunleye, all of my sisters (their families) and brothers (both extended & immediate).. my darling sister, Princess Tope Akinkuotu and husband... a huge thank you. Without you all, I could not have finished this great writing adventure.

To all of my friends... you know who you are... you are cherished. Big kudos to all of my reviewers and bloggers.... I owe you a debt of gratitude.

.

CONTENTS

ACKNOWLEDGMENTS

To my mentor, Dr. Kathleen McCoy my, I want to
 thank you for your continuous support in all of my
endeavors. You are a true gem. My Brandman
University classmates, and all of the professors; you
have truly blessed my life with your strength

All successful people (men and women) are big dreamers. They imagine what their future could be, ideal in every respect, and then they work every day toward their distant vision, that goal, or purpose.

Brian Tracy

"For I know the plans I have for you," says the LORD. "They are plans for good and not for disaster, to give you a future and a hope".

New Living Translation © 2007

PRINCESS FUMI STEPHANIE HANCOCK, BSN, M.A., Ph.D.

PRAISES FOR PRINCESS FUMI'S BOOKS

Fumi Hancock is an incredible woman with an incredible passion to see people, women and men alike fulfill their purpose on this earth. She has witnessed first-hand in her own life, and in the lives of friends and family, huge circumstances and challenges that have come to distract and derail them from the plan and purpose that God has created them for.

As you read, I believe you will be freed to dream once again. You will gain a heart-felt determination to become all YOU are intended to be and be moved to action to finish your race despite all odds." **~Pastor Janet Conley, Snr. Pastor – Cottonwood Christian Center, Los Alamitos, California.**

"With hopes of healing herself and helping others, Fumi writes these words of inspiration to others" **~Lynn Miller, West Windsor & Plainsboro Newspaper**

"Fumi shares the message of hope in the midst of tragedy."
~ **Star Ledger**

"Fumi is a breath of fresh air to those who cannot see their way out and have lost hope. She is a modern day Esther understanding her past, recognizing her season and God's timing, while embracing her future. She reigns supreme as a communicator, a visionary, a spiritual giant that the world is about to discover, only we knew it all along."~ **Dr. Phyllis Carter Pole, Author: Temperament – Your Spiritual DNA.**

November 2012, Fumi Hancock's first young adult fantasy novel, The Adventures of Jewel Cardwell: *Hydra's Nest* became **an amazon bestseller.**
PICK UP YOUR COPY: http://www.amazon.com/Fumi-Hancock/e/B009BHBI6S

Spring Hill resident Fumi Hancock has been riding a wave of success since her new book, The Adventures of Jewel Cardwell: Hydra's Nest hit the shelves in September 2012
~**The Advertisers' News- Spring Hill**

PRAISES FOR PRINCESS FUMI HANCOCK'S US BASED TV SHOW THE PRINCESS IN SUBURBIA TV (AN INNOVATIVE & INSPIRATIONAL LIFESTYLE TALK SHOW) WWW.THEPRINCESSINSUBURBIA.COM

Welcome to
The Princess of Suburbia's Haven

Snicker or Cry as this Suburbia Goddess Shares Her Life Story & Dishes Out Spicy Recipes for Life, Love, Family & Everything Inbetween!

www.twitter.com/PrincessinSub;   www.theprincessinsuburbia.blogspot.com
http://www.youtube.com/user/PrincessinSuburbia

Despite our bad international image, some Nigerians, like Dr. Fumi Hancock, still believe in promoting our image and African culture through her online TV Show. Bravo! ~
Prince AF

OMG just realized you have lots of videos, before and after this. I am off to watch them all ~**CY**

I really enjoyed one of your videos some minutes ago

online. Keep the fire of good work you are doing burning, you are a source of inspiration to me and my family, God will increase your knowledge ~ **SO**

I am a new fan of the Princess in Suburbia Show!~ **Fl**

Didn't realize you had other episodes. Just got back from your channel. I am a new fan!~**LS**

I don't know how to thank you for your activities and your online tv programming. God will continue to strengthen your ability, provide more grease to your elbow ~ **OB**

You are so funny princess. You make me laugh so much ~ **RV**

I love your laughter and the way you approach life, princess ~ **EB**

More grease to your elbow, princess in suburbia. I will keep watching ~ **GL**

Just found your video and I loved it. I am off to watch others on your channel ~**JL**

I came across your channel, Princess in Suburbia USA and found the content to be quite engaging and empowering. Thank you for making us laugh ~**YS**

Your show and the Let's Go Innovate Africa group online is quite inspiring. I am happy to be a part of this movement ~ **KC**

"Upanishad"

…sitting at the feet of the master…

PRINCESS FUMI STEPHANIE HANCOCK, BSN, M.A., Ph.D.

PREFACE

If you are looking for a get rich quick gimmick; THIS IS NOT IT! Everything we do in life takes consistently working at it. I take this time to appeal to you that if you have taken the first step to purchase this book; give the information a chance to get rooted inside of you before drawing your conclusions. In addition, I ask for your fairness – as once this is purchased, you really can't return it, can you? Respecting other people's hard work is the beginning of achieving yours too, right too?.

A parked car will never go anywhere; it doesn't matter how much you desire it to move! It WILL NEVER MOVE, unless you move it!

Having said that, I am glad you have chosen to pick up this

book and hopefully it will prod you into picking up the other books in the series of 2RespectMyLife ©2013. The concepts discussed therein, though they may seem simplistic to some, actually work.

Twenty years ago, I interviewed an extremely wealthy man: He was wealthy in all areas of life. His children were respectful, doing great in school, his relationship with his immediate family – wife and children as well as his extended family were something I aspired for; his businesses were just booming incredibly and globally at that--- he was just an all-around successful man; not perfect but one with a great head on his shoulder, well rounded that is.

When he finally agreed to see me, I was elated… ready to immerse myself in what he had to tell me. I asked him what his secrets to success and generating wealth were. Like many would – I was looking for something incredibly deep … a seemingly complicated equation to his success.

After the interview was over, I walked away from him thinking how simplistic his answers were. Needless to say, I was extremely disappointed and a tad-bit offended to have wasted all those time with the man! His simple answers made me feel like someone was playing a practical joke on me and there was a camera in a secret place waiting to film my flawed life. I did not heed his advice because it just seemed so uncomplicated and I couldn't wrap my mind around how just taking those simple steps (on a daily basis) would yield success to more or less generate wealth. You see, I was looking and waiting for a thunder-bolt response from this man; I needed something to shake me loose from whatever was holding on to me and what was ensuring I stayed in hopelessness, despair and frustration~ relentlessly working hard and never really garnering any great achievements in return. His last words to me were, "whatever happens to you, NEVER GET DESPERATE FOR ANYTHING! It will always cloud your judgment. Secondly, it really doesn't matter what field or industry you choose to start your life journey, even if it were as a clergy man or someone who runs a non-profit organization (NGO) - just make the effort to apply these simple steps. They will be your lifeline in dealing with every aspect of your life."

You are probably eager to know what these impartations are… I just mentioned two of them earlier. Argh! Here is what I garnered from that meeting: Whatever mistakes you made yesterday has since passed… you cannot bring yesterday back, likewise, you should not repeat yesterday's mistake today. Today is a new day. You have been given a new canvas to write on, a second chance to make something great out of your life canvas. Now today, choose wisely. More importantly, while on the journey of discovering your life's mission, regardless of what you may be going through, live life with ***passion*** and ***intentional gratitude***. These two elements unlock the keys to your success; they will turn a beggar into a wealthy person; a nobody into a well-known Innovative Star Player ™. It will literally change your atmosphere and prepare you for successful living. Being intentional means making a conscious choice on a daily basis to make a change either within ourselves or to be a change maker in our environment. We as beings made in God's image with all of the power and dominion, we have the authority to call things into existence.

Have you ever consistently talked about fear of a particular situation until that which you talked about manifested? I know I have. I remember at the age of 11, when I was in boarding school in a rural part of Nigeria. I had not seen my parents or my friends for months and I was desperate. I watched as some of my friends' who had family in close vicinity went to their homes for short breaks while I stayed at the boarding school. One day I came up with a temporary fix, I was going to send the word to my parents and my friends who were over 800 miles away that I was very sick. I figured, if anything would get to my family that would be the message to do it. Without remorse, I set my plan in motion, sent the word out and waited to see the reaction of my family. Well, as predicted, in flooded my whole clan into the community where my boarding school was. However, what would have turned out to be a great visit turned sour that afternoon. I had gotten out of bed and began feeling woozy! I wasn't sure what the problem was. I quickly concluded that I was probably hungry. Only this illness did not go away after my lunch. By the time evening rolled in, I was under my sheets shivering like a chicken about to be slaughtered. The sweat pouring down my body had painted the bed sheets greenish yellow. By the time my parents got to my room, I was already hallucinating. I was gravely ill. At the end of the whole situation, I ended up missing a semester as I was sick with fever, extremely weak and in excruciating pain from all the doctor's injection sites punctures all over my body. I was told I had lain in bed for about three months before I came through. I woke up thinking, never in my life would I call illness or anything evil nor would I even entertain the thought in my head ever again. While I can't say for sure if there was a correlation between my illness and the word I had sent out that morning, here is a valuable lesson to learn: You must continually declare positive words upon your life, the lives of those around you and more importantly upon your ventures. If you wake up every morning and what comes out of your mouth is how tired you are, you will be tired. It is that simple! The moral learned from this experience was a great affirmation of the rich wise man's words to me about desperation.

Twenty something years later from the time I had the interview with the wise man, and still brutally anchored to my series of failed ventures, a stack of disappointments, and broken relationships … I FINALLY GOT IT! Alas, I finally understood what the wise rich man was saying. I now realized that there are gems in the very small packages which come our way. We have to be careful not to dismiss what does not look, sound or smell like we anticipated. SUCCESS is not really a difficult concept if we try to adapt ourselves to its rules. The problem occurs when we are so hung up on our own self; we want things our way, when we want it and how we want it. The syndrome of thinking the world owes us anything has become the order of the day. Life is quickly eroding from the concept of working hard for something, appreciating the people you pass along the way and celebrating your success with gratitude on a daily basis. Now, we have "half-baked" people with half-baked ideas or even stolen ideas roaming the streets. It is my prayer that you would not be a part of that sanity and that you will arise and live your life to the fullest but more importantly, with authenticity.

A GREAT LIFE LESSON LEARNED: While I was struggling to make things happen for me...I forgot the cardinal rule... enjoy yourself while climbing the ladder. You only live once and once today becomes yesterday, you can never re-capture it. What you do today matters! Good or bad. The decisions you make today will ultimately steer you in one of these directions: The path to consistent victory or the wide highway to disaster. It doesn't matter what you think your vision or passion is, if you do not get up and do something about it, it will remain dormant. I share this to let you know that after you have worked your way through this poignant experience of discovering your vision and holding the torch high for the world to see, the action that must follow will eventually chart the course of your life's boat.

Well then, if you are ready to steer your boat gallantly, understanding that parts of this adventure will force you to face both the negative and positive paths you have once treaded and dreaded, you are in the right place, at the right time, the right season and the day of total immersion into this discovery adventure!

While you may nudge me to play a little nice with some topics, friends, colleagues and family know this about me, I will tell it like it is...I will not add to the word or subtract from it because I WANT YOU TO SUCCEED! Hear this, this is your journey. You get to write or re-write your life story. It is ultimately up to you what story you choose to write in the book of your life. This book is packed with nuggets of wisdom and as I open my wisdom vault for you to partake of, it is important that you unveil your eyes so the life lessons can be deeply rooted to yield great fruits.

In this book, Your Vision Torch: An Innovator's Prescription for Igniting Your Dreams & Harnessing Your Vision, we will explore the following:

How to clean your house and rid yourself of toxic situations, people and environment;

Debunking the battle field and raging warzone within;

Addressing the Good, the Bad and the Ugly of ones' circumstances.;

Examining the qualities of a great innovative leader; tapping into the "muscle mass" of your vision;

Developing an effective roadmap and providing an innovative leadership physician's prescription to igniting and harnessing your vision;

Provision of the essential vision impacting cardinal rules and failure arsenal weapon, governing the harnessing of your vision;

Unveiling the vision success model to help you live your best life and live authentically at that. So, be vigilant, be attentive, and BE READY for a radical change. Let's roll!

Whatever the mind of man (or woman) can conceive and believe, it can achieve.

Napoleon Hill

Once Upon a Time ....

Write Your Own Story....

Life is a song – sing it. Life is a game – play it. Life is a challenge – meet it. Life is a dream – realize it. Life is a sacrifice – offer it. Life is love – enjoy it.

Sai Baba

PRINCESS FUMI STEPHANIE HANCOCK, BSN, M.A., Ph.D.

WRITE YOUR OWN STORY NOW!....

WHAT DO YOU BELIEVE TO BE TRUE ABOUT
YOUR LIFE, YOUR RELATIONSHIPS, YOUR
ASPIRATIONS ETC? JUST DESCRIBE WHO YOU
THINK YOU ARE ON THIS PAGE. DO NOT HOLD
BACK AND WRITE AS MUCH INFORMATION AS
IT FLOWS THROUGH YOU: GOOD OR WHAT YOU
PERCEIVE TO BE BAD. LET'S GO!

A guy who is seeking fulfillment
through my purpose. Insecure, sensitive,
introverted. Lazy and often distracted.
Eagerly wanting to succeed and reach
my potential. Loving and genuine.
Needs to be pushed more a encouraged
and needs that hunger fire (Zeal)
and courage to apply the abundance
of knowledge that he knows towards
reality. Everything will be released
from within you all in due time. Slow
and steady wins the race.

----

1 HOUSECLEANING

If you are still with me, I welcome you to the rest of your life where everything visible and invisible is possible! In literal terms, house cleaning is not usually a fun event. If you are like me, there have been times when you just don't feel like dealing with cleaning your house; unless of course if you have a compulsive disorder which compels you to constantly clean your environment. At any rate, it is crucial that we take a look at who we are, what we have accomplished thus far, mistakes made in the past but most importantly, what do we perceive as our pay off when we steer our lives in the wrong direction? In life, we are usually driven by two emotions, pain or pleasure.

As part of cleaning your house, you are also required to get your minds ready for extensive stretching and education. I urge you to keep the following words in your fore-front as you progress on this journey; begin to ask yourself these questions " what do these words mean to me? How would I define them?"

Innovation	**Dreams**	**Vision**	**Ignite**
Harness	**Torch**	**Roadmap**	**Blueprint**

Innovation ~ The introduction of something new. That is, a new idea, method or way of doing things. In addition, it can also refer to an improvement to something already in existence Merriam-Webster (m-w.com, 2013). Innovators generate and execute dreams. They are constantly looking for ways and opportunities where ideas merge. You can either row your life's boat with no passion or get up and be somebody! My hope is that you will do the latter by letting me help you clean house. The intent of doing this exercise is not to make you dwell in your past failures but to help you move forward in a strong and affirmative way. There is no way we can clean up our act now without looking at past events. When we summon the courage to face our past, and then tailor it where it truly belongs; we start our success path in a strong manner. "If you're not failing every now and again, it's a sign you're not doing anything very innovative" ~Woody Allen; something to think about the next time your mind accuse you of your past failures.

(1) Take this time to jot down all the ideas you have ever had. Remember, no idea or thought is silly. A perfect example is Facebook, which at its conception was dubbed one of the most ridiculous start-up ideas (Wolfe, Quora.com, 2013)! Can you believe it? Now, it has literally become a household name. So, here we go....

(a). Those ideas that you considered a total bust. That is, a failure:

(b). Those ideas in which you enjoyed marginal success:

(c). Those ideas where you succeeded and considered it a slam dunk! That is, your success was incredible:

(d). Those ideas you have yet to accomplish:

What are the stumbling blocks you can identify for not pursuing those ideas you have yet to accomplish? A dream doesn't become reality through magic; it takes sweat, determination and hard work - Colin Powell. A dream does not manifest because you have an epiphany. It manifests if and when you are indeed ready for its grand entrance. I love Eleanor Roosevelt's statement that is as follows: "The future belongs to those who believe in the beauty of their dreams."

Examine what pair of glasses you are wearing today? Is it making you see only disgust and impossibilities or is it constantly showing you the bright future you have despite your challenges? Only you can steer your boat and whichever way you steer it, it will determine your final destination. My role as your innovation life coach and business / leadership strategist is to help you get on the right path; to present to you a unique approach in mapping your vision and not only that, empower you by providing this book as a tool and a guide to gauging or measuring your success.

Here are other thought provoking nuggets straight from my exclusive wisdom vault, what is your belief about your aspiration today? Do you allow your present circumstances to dictate it or do you trust God at his word and still move through the hardship of life towards it? What is your dream today and what are your aspirations? Do you have enough faith to back it up even when society or your surrounding is screaming "No? Not you! It can never happen to you!"

Be encouraged today and know that it doesn't matter what man says, if God says it, it is finished! Settled! Completed! The participation needed is YOURS not that of your nay-sayers! Do you know that something good can still come out of that unbearable circumstance... do you know that something great can still come out of the country where you are living right now? You are a powerful force to contend with and that is why all hell has broken loose around you... You carry your creator's gene pool... the vision for the world, you are powerful... you are resilient... YOU ARE. You must bear the negative to ensure that you will carry "your vision" to term without abortion! Get ready to birth your vision, in-spite of... When God gave you a vision, he didn't tell you it will never happen because you don't have the money! Or because of where you were born! HE SIMPLY GAVE YOU THE VISION! So all you need do is move in obedience and allow him to sort the rest out. FAVOR WILL TAKE YOU WHERE MONEY WILL NEVER TAKE YOU. Now you move into your destiny and place of honor today.

The following exercises are not meant to show you how much of focus you have lost but to encourage you because great innovations are often developed out of ideas that do not match. I have also since learned that no idea is a lost cause; like-wise no experience is a total failure. It is amazing how when the student is ready, the teacher shows up. Life is a journey and an experience. While there are few things we do not have control over; there are many things or occurrences we can change or we can choose to ignore them.

Here is some candid food for thought for you today: What have you chosen to ignore recently or a while back in your life? And if you had a second chance, how would you tackle the issue? One nugget of wisdom I have learned through the years is that often, great things come in small packages... do not despise your humble beginnings... they essentially shape your future too.

Now, let's go back to the list of ideas you shared earlier on; take a hard look at these ideas you have written down? Can you figure out if they meet at some juncture? Or are these ideas so far apart, they are enough to make your head spin?

Can you mention what new idea(s) you recently came up with? If it was not totally new, what idea(s) have you approached in a different way that brought about innovation?

----

(2). Are you moving forward with this idea(s)? If not, why not? That is, what do you consider as the barrier to not moving forward with that dream?

Dreams ~ The word "dream" has different connotations, that is, depending on what you are referring to, it could mean successions of images, ideas, emotions and sensations that occur during certain stages of sleep (thefreedictionary.com). While this is so, in this book I am making reference to a totally different concept. One which is tied to your destiny, vision, mission and goal in life. That is, your heart beat… your heart's desire, its hopes and aspirations.

Now, let's go a little down memory lane, shall we? I need you to think back to when you were the ages mentioned here. For some of you, this may elicit pain while others, a joyful time. Either way, the goal is to be able to delve into our past to see what truth lies buried therein. Many times, we can see how we have been derailed or perhaps derailed ourselves from the destiny we were meant to live. Often, life happens and we find ourselves in the "survival" mode that we bury our heart desire just so we can live another trying day! I will share my personal story with you. Ever since I was little, I knew I was called to help others… to restore them and bring them back to quality health. I also knew that somehow writing would be the vehicle for this restoration. More importantly, I knew there was a mantle of leadership in the political realm. However, when I immigrated to the Unites States of America as an African Princess trying to adapt, I found myself sucked into the rat race … running profusely against time and attempting to survive. I felt constantly spent, emotionally, physically and mentally. In the midst of this chaos, I forgot or perhaps buried what I knew to be true about myself.

Can you remember what you imagined you would become when you were:

5 years old?

----

10 years old?

----

15 years old?

Over 20 years old?

Let me ask a sticky question... for today... What do you do? (i.e. your job description/career wise)

How far away or close are you to what you had defined above, as what you thought you were going to be?

Vision ~ While "vision" is also defined in different ways, I need you to focus on this definition: The stated aims and objectives of a business or person; the ability or an instance of great perception, especially of future developments; a person of vision. It is the act or power of anticipating that which will or may come to be (dictionary.reference.com).

Vision execution requires perception and discernment with imaginative conception. Where there is no vision, people perish. Likewise, where there is no vision, it doesn't matter what you are trying to do or become, NOTHING WILL WORK! Your life journey must start with a vision. Often, our vision may be obscured due to life challenges but those who persevere and pull through the challenges, victory awaits at the end. Habakkuk 2:2- And the Lord answered me" write the vision; make it plain on tablets, as he may run who reads it." (American Standard Bible, 1995). Dreams pass into the reality of action. From the actions stem the dream again; and this interdependence produces the highest form of living (Anais Nni).

Ignite ~ This is a powerful word that's worthy of study. The free Dictionary (2013) defines it as "to cause to burn. That is to set fire to something. To begin to burn and glow." Know this, it will take faith, trust, and relentless tenacity to pull your vision into existence. This will entail you torching or igniting that which is within you already. The other side of the coin is ensuring that you too are ignitable. As an ignitable soul, you were born to set dreams on fire and ablaze!

What role have you been playing in the scheme of things? Have you set ablaze your dream? Is your passion still intact? Or have you allowed your ideas to lay dormant and you can't seem to find your way out of complacency? Our dreams begin with responsibilities to ourselves, the dream itself and those who will partake of that dream. "So many of our dreams at first seem improbable, and then, when we summon the will, they soon become inevitable – Christopher Reeves.

It doesn't matter how many times your gut confirms your destiny to you; if you do not participate in ensuring its fruition, it will never happen.

Vision Torch is a phenomenal arsenal to attack the camp of your enemy. It is one thing to finally get the vision, it is another to ignite it. However, in between our vision and the actual ignition; we need a tool that ties them together neatly. This is the Torch, otherwise known as vision mapping.

Many of us are running around in circles, we desperately want to ignite our passion and vision but the missing link is keeping us from reaching our full potential. Without the torch, which helps in setting the "fire," failure is inevitable. The Torch is a "reservoir" for your vision as well as the fire used in setting the vision ablaze.

Harness ~ Macmillan Dictionary (2013) defines Harness as to get control of something to use it for a particular purpose. When harnessing, our ultimate goal is to aim to do better by having control of our skills and talents. Harnessing also requires that you make better use of "something" of value. Hence, the reason for using the word harness in this book's sub-title. As you progress along in this journey, you will learn how to harness your visions and ignite your dreams. Both work hand in hand. For you to harness something of substance, you must take the time to understand the character of that which you are intending to harness. Many of us have a vague idea of our vision but very few are absolutely clear on what they should do. When you have a clear understanding of who you are and what you need to be doing, then you do not have to push hard to place yourself in someone else's lane. You simply appreciate the gift bestowed upon you; learn to drive in your lane, and most importantly, YOU WILL LEARN TO WAIT YOUR TURN! In addition, harnessing ones vision requires inner strength, loads of wisdom, an incredible amount of discernment and learning to know when to launch out powerfully. Many have aborted their vision in the wrong place, at the wrong time and with the wrong person because they have not learned to be still. Part of maturity is also learning to understand that there is a season for everything and that because a person close to you may be operating under an open heaven it means that same heaven is open to you. Although I cannot deny the power of association; a topic I fully addressed in one of my books, *Who is in your life boat? The Dream Maker or the Dream Breaker: The Clown who occupies Your Circle of Influence* (will be released soon but please keep checking my website for updates).

Roadmap ~Often, when I use a roadmap I interchange it with a blueprint. What comes to your mind when you think of a roadmap or a blueprint? Merriam-Webster dictionary (2013) defines it as a detailed plan to guide progress toward a goal. Plans fail when there is no plan. Many go through life with no definitive plan and they often wonder what went wrong when there is an obstruction in their way of living. We live in a day and age filled with incredible amounts of uncertainty. It therefore behooves us to at least set concrete plans in motion to avert problems as best as we can. A blueprint is a plan. It essentially dictates your direction, guides you and shows you the next step in life. A blueprint is a design or drawn up plan. The great component of a blueprint is the fact that it is not rigid but flexible. Though it is meant to show you the way, you are not expected to become enslaved to it. With the blueprint to any plan, it has the capacity to be incredibly flexible and adaptable. Either you run the day, or the day runs you- Jim Rohn. You stand the chance of being run by the day when you don't have a plan. It is therefore crucial that plans are put in place no matter how little they are. Plans move one from spot A to spot B. Our job is to be bold enough to follow the path laid ahead of us by the blueprint, even when it means leaving behind what one is most familiar with.

Even though we may have dictionary interpretations of these words, when adapted personally, there is the tendency to either stretch their meanings a little further to suit our own needs or to mentally delete certain aspects of their meaning if they cause us pain. Regardless of what pain we may derive from merely thinking about these words, we must be determined to cut through that pain and usher in our freedom… freedom to finally accomplish our life mission and the vision we know we were meant to achieve. As we journey on, please write down all the ***bolded and italicized words*** you encounter. There is a method to this madness…. Just hang in there.

Questions I need you to consider before moving forward with this process. Please do not attempt to skip any of these exercises as they will assist you in moving forward with your vision successfully:

(1). If a stranger came up to you today and asked you this question, ***who are you?*** How would you respond?

2(a).What are the three words which you believe define and describe who you are?

2(b) Why have you chosen these words to describe who you are?

2(c) Do you know the dictionary definitions of your chosen words? And what are they?

2(d) How close are these definitions to your personal beliefs of who you think you are?

---

3. What role do you believe your ***background, relationships (past & present)*** and your ***convictions*** play in your choice of words?

I don't know about you but if I hear one more person ask me what do I do?, I believe I just might blow a gasket!. How many times have we heard people ask us this coming question and how many times have we answered the same question differently?

4. What if this same stranger turned around and asked another question, **what do you do?**

It will be interesting to see how you describe or define yourself. There are few things you would observe here, that you are one of those who define themselves by what they do, that is, their career, while some define themselves by the role they have within their home, while others are simply confused and not sure how to define themselves. These are certainly cracks in our lives that need to be cleaned out.

Once Upon a Time ….

Life is a PUZZLE. Tell me what fits in yours….

Don't judge each day by the harvest you reap but by the seeds you plant.

Robert Louis Stevenson

2 VISIBLE AND INVINCIBLE

LIFE IS WHAT YOU MAKE OF IT!
Write Your Story Well and Make it Plain

Now that we have made the effort to clean the junk in our backyards by taking a hard look at "our issues of life", it is important that we begin to debunk the lies ruminating in our heads. To succeed, your desire for success should be greater than your fear of failure- Bill Cosby.

Someone once asked me how to overcome the feeling of failure… how do you get beyond failure when all you have experienced are rolls of successive failure? I would be lying if I told you I could cure any of those feelings. In fact, the truth is that when you wake up every day, your mind goes to war … between telling yourself you will make it and your surroundings constantly reminding you that you will never make it. This is what I term the battle of the mind. The pivotal question then is how do we debunk the lies our minds tell us on a daily basis? How do we push through the war zone called "mind" and move into our destiny? In the midst of these mind battles, are we able to see clearly what we are meant to do or be? As much as many of us may want to bury our heads in the sand and just pray our way through without any actions on our part, it is vital that to overcome the battle in our minds, a request must be proactive. As religious creatures, we have the tendency to hide behind religion and hope that religion would make choices for us. The truth is that religion is a guide … in essence, a lamp to guide our feet. Ultimately, we must make our decisions and take action to activate what we know to be true. Believe you can and you are halfway there – Theodore Roosevelt. There is a popular saying; you can always make lemonade out of lemons! Every moment and every event of every man's life on earth plants something in his soul – Thomas Merton. What are you planting into your life? What seeds are you sowing that are now germinating? Believe that lie is worth living and your belief will help create the fact – William James.

When thinking about these words "Visible" and "Invincible", I thought of faith. We have all heard the popular scripture, Faith is the substance of things hoped for, the evidence of things yet unseen." I can't remember how many times I have quoted and heard people quote that scripture. Yet this same scripture could potentially be one that is often ignored, in particular, in times of trial. When thought of deeply, it alludes to the fact that visibility often does not require much faith as you see, you believe… but argh the invisible or invincible will stretch our faith to the max.. This is where the challenges often manifest. Not only will exercising faith stretch us to the max, particularly when our surroundings and everything within us tells us it is impossible. How can you start a business with nothing to your name? How can you move forward when all who you expect to help won't even stand up to be counted? How can I? How can this be possible? How can…..

Life is a dream for the wise, a game for the fool, a comedy for the rich, a tragedy for the poor—Sholom Alechem. This phrase is all dependent on what you perceive life to be. After all, beauty is in the eye of the beholder. You will never grow past what you see or perceive yourself to be. Regardless of my effort in wanting you to success, if you don't want it bad enough, it will not happen. A big lesson I was taught through the years, I can never want something way more than the person involve wants it. It doesn't matter how desperate I want my son to be a medical doctor, if he does not have the desire… it won't happen! A very popular adage, you can lead a horse to the water but you can never force him to drink. For you to accomplish your life goals and mission, you must set a pace for yourself to walk in its direction. In other words, you must make a decision to be an avid participant in writing your own story. I can't write it for you, neither can you parents or brothers or sister. You have to make the conscientious effort at it. How far you go in life depends on your being tender with the young, compassionate with the ages, sympathetic with the striving and tolerant of the weak and strong. Because someday in your life, you will have been all of these – George Washington Carver. Besides, you never know if an angel is right around the corner to help usher you into your destiny.

Life is what YOU MAKE OF IT. Likewise, experience is not what happens to you; it's what you do with what happens to you – Aldous Huxley; great words from the wise. In everything we do, we must strive to make a difference and leave an indelible mark. So while our mind is screaming all things are impossible, as we begin to move towards debunking those lies in our minds, life will take on a different meaning… and a great one at that. So, how do we go about starting this process?

First, **Debunk the battle field and war zone** in your mind. Because it is logical that our minds when we wake up often thinks of ways to remind us that we are a failure; it is important that we trick it to begin thinking otherwise.

The only true wisdom is in knowing you know nothing – Socrates. We are a canvas for the master creator to write on. Great wisdom lies in us understanding that we are nothing without the divine one; that we were divinely created I his image; that we are no imitation but uniquely designed for his great pleasure. That we have control over our thoughts, minds and ways of living. We must acknowledge that to accomplish our goals in life, we must not only exercise patience, love, compassion for one another but firm discipline… as discipline is the bridge between goals and accomplishment – Jim Rohn.

Here are steps we must take to debunk the lies ringing in our heads about our vision.

(1). **Assess the war zone** (either physical or "in the mind") that you may be experiencing right now: **BE TRUTHFUL**. Healing and restoration begins with that.

What are your current war-zone(s) experience? In other words, define what you perceive as your immediate battle(s):

Physical:

Mental/Emotional:

Career/Business:

Other:

Your War-zone Barometer™:

This is where I need you to pull out your imaginary barometer, to seriously assess your condition(s): Tell me all about it….Write down all of the emotions you are going through right now, both good, bad and ugly. Remember this is your story… this is a page in your journal and however you may feel, you do not owe anyone explanations. This is simply you getting to the root of it all. **Remember, *write Your Story and Make it plain*.**

Gauge your weapon of war if you have one: What do you know you have via way of fighting the war in your head? Scriptures? Inspirational or motivational quotes? Life experiences? Stories your mother told you? What do you have in your wardrobe to help debunk the myths about who you are, warring in your head or mind? No one goes to war without preparation. Likewise in life, you must have a strategy to overcome your mindset, if they are negative ones. This strategy once ironed out will actually help you move on the right path too. So, my question again, what do you carry inside of you that can help you to overcome when the mind sets in to cast aspersions on your abilities?

ENDEARING NUGGETS OF WISDOM FROM MY VAULT TO HELP YOU ON THIS DISCOVERY JOURNEY:

Only a fool goes to war without ammunition. Begin to access your ammunition right now, no matter how small it may seem. Remember the story of David and Goliath (1 Samuel 17 NIV). Goliath, by all standards, was well known as a champion; he was over nine feet tall! He was a man of war, always prepared with bronze helmet to shield his head, wore a coat of scale armor of bronze which weighed five thousand shekels; on his legs Goliath wore bronze greaves; and a bronze javelin was slung on his back! Nobody dared to cross his path. His spear shaft was like a weaver's rod, and its iron point weighed six hundred shekels. Not only was he loaded with arsenal tools, his shield bearer always went ahead of him. Goliath was so confident in his strength, his abilities and his tools that he proudly threw out a challenge! That was his first mistake. You never judge a book by its cover! (Anonymous). There is always a fresh new anointing for our daily walk and if we stay close to the source, the giver of life and ideas, he will continually pour out this anointing, over flowing the brim as he prods us along the path we should be on. Knowing the accolades Goliath had, all the Israelites (Saul included) became terrified as Goliath declared that if he killed the man chosen, Saul and the Israelites would become his property! But so little did he know that his nemesis was on his way.

God knows how to put us in our place when we are getting carried away. David, who was merely a cattle herder, appeared in season: at the right place, at the right time with the right tools! He heard the gifts that would be bestowed upon anyone who defeated Goliath. While everyone shivered, David walked confident in the Lord! His desire to be the WINNER of the announced prizes: The King would give the person who kills Goliath great wealth; he will also marry the king's daughter and his family exempted from taxes! His vision was too large for a cattle herder, but it was big enough to drive him to want to try. Isn't it amazing that in the midst of cattle, David was being prepared for the greatest battle of his life… one which would ultimately change the course of his life.

There is a lesson here… sometimes we find ourselves in positions that do not make sense. We are frustrated and completely depleted, stretched to the full capacity our brain can contain; we keep telling ourselves we don't belong there and that the position was possibly lower than expected. Out of this small experience comes the power, the tool to win the race! David's ability to kill Goliath was undermined by his brothers and perhaps others in the crowds who were looking at his weight and height in comparison to Goliaths'. If they were anything like me, I would probably have gone to find his family, asked them to come quickly and take him to a psychiatric ward! David confidently envisioned his previous experiences with lions and bears. He did not look at Goliath's size but knew that what he carried, no matter how small and insignificant it might look on the outside. He was confident and if he doubted for even a second, he did not let it show. Amidst the noise from people probably telling him he was crazy to want to attempt a deadly fight, David was focused and, with a sling and a stone, he defeated the great Goliath! One stone changed the course of his life! Use whatever you have, since it can change the course of your life if you choose to maximize its use!... *Just a sling and a stone....*

WHAT IS THE SLING AND STONE IN YOUR LIFE? WHAT IS THAT WEAPON OF WARFARE YOU HAVE TUCKED AWAY? USE THIS SPOT TO JOT DOWN WHAT YOU HAVE... BE IT A SCRIPTURE OR INSPIRATIONAL WORDS FROM A WELL RESPECTED PERSON.

VISIBLE is defined as "capable of being seen." – m-w.com.

What do you see right now as part of your future? Pain or pleasure? Please provide examples here of either/ or/both?

INVINCIBLE is defined as "too powerful to be defeated or overcome. That is, insurmountable, unconquerable or unbeatable" – thefreedictionary.com. What do you perceive as being invincible in your life today?

PRINCESS FUMI STEPHANIE HANCOCK, BSN, M.A., Ph.D.

Imagery and **Words** which make you go….*Ummmmm*….

Demystifying **Life's Puzzle**

This is a fun board for you to play with. Stretch your imagination as you begin to think deeply on these words or phrases.

Image courtesy of Danilo Rizzuti at FreeDigitalPhotos.net

What's **Fire** & the **Torch** Got to Do with it!

Igniting Your **Dreams**   **Harnessing** Your **Vision**

to catch fire   to suffocate   close association
to heat up   to quench to put out   to misapply
a state of mind marked by abstraction   to extinguish
a visionary creation of the imagination   something seen in
a dream   to direct a cause in your favor   to begin to
glow   to apply   to set afire   to misuse   to set in
motion   **the act or power of imagination**

Variations in Life's Gifts

Take a close look at the following imagery and write down *what you see and what does this mean to you.*

Courtesy of the Princess of Suburbia ™, Dr. Fumi. Hancock

Keep writing. I need for you to describe exactly what you see. That is, the first thought which came to your mind ... not the second or the third. And don't be afraid or ashamed to write down exactly the feelings elicited by this picture. Remember, THIS IS YOUR STORY! And you are the driver of this life boat. How you steer it, that is, how you steer your mind is solely your responsibility. We only get free from what we work at judiciously. So, let's roll WE ARE KEEPING IT REAL HERE.

My thought on this exercise:

Depending on how you perceive your challenges, there are often variations in our experiences which color our over perspective of life. While some may see a glass as half empty, others may see that very same glass as half full. IT IS

ALL IN ONES PERSPECTIVE. In addition, when you take a look at the imagery above and what you have written; what can you deduce from your thought process?

Some may take a look at these pictures and see abject poverty, which in turn would elicit either pity, compassion, sadness or/and love and anger that anyone would live in such a place. Interestingly, few who may be living in similar circumstances may look at it as a "safe haven" as this is all they know. Either way, no single feeling elicited is the right one. What is important to note here is that whatever feelings that are elicited by these imagery will ultimately drive the actions we take.

APPLICATION TO YOUR VISION TORCH: The type of mirror you pick up to **examine your current state or circumstance; the type of mirror you pick up to gauge what you believe you are called to do will ultimately drive** not only how you perceive your vision but will dictate how you push through to accomplish that vision or goal. In other words, if your reaction to the imagery set before you as your vision torch is pain and compassion as I suspect it would in some people, these emotions will drive you to wither succeed or self-destruct. You will either be driven to push through with strong conviction and determination to get over the pain thus reaching your mission, vision or/and goal. The other side of the coin is that these same emotions may cause some people to become catatonic, eliciting more self-pity as they reminisce, remembering their own situation. When this is in motion, said people do not go very far with their vision. In fact, more often than not, they move from one struggle to the other, and never accomplish or finish anything and are always looking for the next best thing or quick fix. It is my hope that you are not one of those. And if this exercise has caused you to truly determine that you may be this type of person…. DO NOT WORRY… YOU ARE IN A *NO JUDGEMENT* ZONE where all things are possible and where you can be set free from such complacency and self-pity. Only those who dare to fail greatly can ever achieve greatness – Robert F Kennedy. Our paths have crossed for a reason; you selection of this book will change the course of your life, if adapted appropriately. When a woman finds herself to be unexpectedly pregnant, it sometimes causes a crisis in her life, depending her environment. Many times that crisis causes her to look for answers outside of herself. Sometimes she is led to the Creator. If, however, she is unable to care for the children the Creator, our heavenly Father, places the child in the care of people He trusts. He picks the right parents for the right child at the right time. What am I saying here? The Creator of the universe did not make a mistake in choosing you to carry that vision neither are you an accident waiting to happen but His pure delight waiting to shine in an extraordinary way. More importantly, you are unique and there is no one on the face of this earth that can implement that with which He has entrusted you. You are valuable and precious! You are extraordinary! You are divinely orchestrated…..YOU ARE…. Here is a great start for you (Check out my eBook: My Destiny's Quill: Effective Life Strategies for Successful People: A DREAMER'S JOURNAL (RESPECT YOUR LIFE SERIES- Amazon).

Fill in the gap…..Just like a young child would do… with innocence and not holding back. Imagine you are this child… look in his or her eyes and complete the following sentence. Write as many accolades as you are inspired to. Find scriptures or inspirational quotes which will help you to define who you are.

Here we go…. **I AM….**

(1). **I am** what God says I am... Precious and divine....
(2). --

For those of you who may be pondering why we do this exercise, please indulge me. You may be like me. At some point in my life and with chaos slowly eroding my self-esteem and pride; I got confused. That is, I found myself in a place where I could not truly identify my vision. I knew I was meant to do something or be somebody, but the weight of life forced the vision way down deep. This exercise, however simple it may sound has helped me on several occasions to get clarity in my decision making. When you get to the chore of determining who you are, you know what you are called to do and you move confidently into it with no reservation. This is why it is important that you write those accolades down of who you are. A very dear friend, a bishop, once said something I would never forget. I have since held on to it and recalled it when life's weight begins to bear down on me... as we all know it will! He said, *I was manufactured in Africa, assembled in USA and dispatched to the world.* What a wonderful way of letting me know how valuable I was not only to my immediate community but to the world at large. Today, I wake up every day just thinking about the statement and moving in that realm of possibilities. You too can achieve this when you start off your day knowing WHO YOU ARE.

What has this exercise taught you or revealed to you about YOU?

What is **visible** today about who you are? That is, what can you and others see about who YOU ARE? E.g. people see and experience my compassionate side because I am constantly helping others to achieve. Because of my compassion for people, I founded a nonprofit US-based (NGO) organization that caters to the needs of children in

Africa. (www.adassafoundation.org).

How is "WHO YOU ARE" visible today?
To date, we have provided scholarships for up to 40 children from the elementary level to college level. In addition, we have provided a state of the art library in my community, Emure Kingdom in Ekiti State Nigeria. Part of bring rooted and operating in ones' vision is also *giving*. Some want to just take while not giving anything in return. This is a wrong foundation for anyone who wants to be successful in life.

Discipline is the Bridge between Goals and Accomplishments -J.Rohn

Now, let's go to you. Hopefully, the exercise I have provided will help you to complete this exercise.
(1). Write down how you believe who you are is visible to you and to the world around you?

What you know:

What people have told you:

----

(2). What is **invisible** about who you are? In other words, who do you know you are that has yet to manifest?

Beauty, they say, is in the eye of the beholder. What pleasures one person may cause pain for another. It's all in **the act and/or power of our imagination.** Few years back, I visited my community, Emure Kingdom with a group of my Tennessee friends. On one of our tours, my royal father, King Emmanuel Adebayo took us to the old palace where my grandfather ruled his people.

Courtesy of the Princess of Suburbia ™, Dr. Fumi. Hancock

While some may look at these pictures and wonder how anyone could have lived in this ancient palace. I, on the other hand, saw history in the making for me. I imagined being in that palace, which has now become a tourist attraction… I saw my inheritance and genealogy. It was overwhelming and completely surreal to be standing next to where my grandfather reigned as the king. King Emmanuel Adebayo told us of a story that was passed on to us by our forefathers… The stone in the picture above emits a certain power and no one has been able to ascertain how it got there. According to the king, when you stand in its presence, it is important that you evidence no hatred for anyone and that you not lie. Often when the king had to deliberate over issues and the cabinet could not determine who was at fault; said person would be brought in the front of that stone that has the curse. Whatever that person said there would come to pass. If he cursed himself that he would die or get hurt. If he did what he was accused of, within the 7 days of his proclamation that which he proclaimed would fall upon him! King Emmanuel Adebayo who is a great leader and a Christian told me it was true! Even though as a Christian he has since brought Christianity to a higher level in Emure kingdom... this act of faith did not however reduce the power which lay dormant in that old palace. Again, it's all in **the act and/or power of our imagination. Visions always begin with a dream.** Have you had one lately? Within our dreams and aspirations, we find our opportunities - Sue Ebaugh

Where are we going with this?

What's fire and torch got to do with it?

Do you know the difference between education and experience? Education is when you read the fine print; experience is what you get when you don't.

Pete Seeger

3 WHO ARE YOU AND WHAT HAVE YOU DONE WITH MY VISION AND MY DREAM?

If you don't challenge yourself, you will never realize what you can become. You can never cross the ocean unless you have the courage to lose sight of the shore – Author Unknown.

Today, I want you to look in the mirror, who do you see steering back at you? At the onset of the preface, chapters 1 & 2; you may have been confused, overwhelmed and perhaps a little desperate to want to know more of what you need to be doing and how you need to execute it. In this chapter, it is my expectation that your answers reflect some changes in your thought patterns about your life purpose. If this doesn't happen yet, don't give up. Keep working on the exercises provided here in this book. Life belongs to the living, and he who lives must be prepared for changes–Johann von Goethe.

I want to talk for a second on *Obscurity vs. Clarity?*

Image courtesy of think4photo at FreeDigitalPhotos.net

When you see this tower, what does it ***instantly*** mean to you?

Let's take a close look at the second picture. ***Write down all what you feel when you look at the following picture.*** I want to know the emotions it elicits as you view it. ***Remember, no feeling is wrong; therefore no reaction is wrong.*** It is all about perspective and you seeing a change in your perspective with life and more importantly in your thought process.

Image courtesy of Dan at FreeDigitalPhotos.net

Dictonary.com (2013) defines obscurity as the state of being unknown. It is also defined as Deficiency or absence of light, darkness. Clarity on the other hand is defined as the quality of being clear or the quality of coherence and intelligibility. With clarity comes light, lucidity and great perception (freedictionary.com). Another way to look at clarity is to experience freedom in ambiguity. In the context of Vision Torch or vision mapping, it clearly means knowing for sure what you are meant to be; deliberately establishing steps to make it happen and finding the courage to pluck all the seeds you had grown earlier on.

Just few weeks ago, I was having problems with my vision. I had neglected this problem for a while because I said to myself I was just too busy to see the eye doctor. Weeks into seeing fuzzy imagery, inability to read instructions well and the undeniable frustration in constantly squinting my eyes; I gave in and went to the eye doctor. In my obscured mind, I could still manage my eyes the way they were over going to sit down at the clinic, attempting to see the eye doctor. I had associated enough pain with sitting at the doctor's office that it took over the rational part of my brain. My thoughts were completely obscured and the pain I envisioned sitting there was greater than any rational decision I could have taken. Whether you think you can or you can't, you're right – Henry Ford.

Image courtesy of Jennifer Ellison at FreeDigitalPhotos.net

The ***Wind of Life*** will always blow. That is a given, that is, a situation or circumstances we have no control over will always surface in our lives for as long as we live. However, your reactions to this wind of life are what matter… this is what will determine your outcome. Every tomorrow has two handles. We can take hold of the handle of anxiety or the handle of faith – Henry Ward Beecher. There is truly nothing new under the sun and there is a time for everything, and a season for every activity under heaven (NIV, Ecclesiastes: 3:1).

Your circumstance is not unique to you. In the same token, we are to take solace in the fact that someone on this planet has the key to our challenge because that person has been through it. Therefore, if they went through it and overcame it, then you can too. No quitter wins anything in life! In life's circumstances, we are always presented with choices: door #1 – QUIT!; door # 2: HOLD ON TO YOUR CREATOR THEN TAKE ACTION; door # 3: DON'T DO ANYTHING! I hear some of us just crying out and quickly wanting out of the circumstance we may be facing. I know I was in that same boat, quickly wanting to get out of my predicament and without bruises. Now I know that the bruises I received are also marks of honor, integrity, and a constant reminder that I made it! So, don't focus on your bruises. They will become marks of honor, strength and valor. As you continue on this journey in this book, carefully consider which door you want to open. It is certainly my hope that by now, hope is arising in you; your faith is being restored and you are garnering for yourself an arsenal to open door # 2.

We must also remember the adage that Rome was not built in a day. As such, we need to quit looking for ways to rush through our experiences. Out of these life experiences come character to sustain our vision. Without character and authenticity, we are doomed to massive failure. It takes time to succeed because success is merely the natural reward of taking time to do anything well – Joseph Ross

When you are at peace, clarity rises up in the midst of your storm and clears the path to success for you. Clarity in vision enables you to be prepared for the road ahead. When you are not clear, you seem scattered; your thoughts are scattered and your decision making process become obscured. That is the wrong time to make any life changing decisions. Therefore, if you go into a battle, YOU MUST BE PREPARED! You cannot afford to be half-baked! On the other hand, having a half-baked idea is not necessarily wrong especially when you take that half-baked idea and work it like your life depended on it… it will move from the realm of potential or the possible, to reality.

Here are the benefits of clarity which I'd like you to ponder as we delve further into this adventure:

> That your Creator has a plan for your life and that this plan is meant to **change the lives** of others too;
> Because of this plan, he has bestowed upon you gifts and your gifts will indeed make room for you;
> **Recognize the season** you are operating under so you don't get frustrated when things are not moving as you'd expected;
> Understand that you are a **sacred being**; extremely gifted **armed with a divine purpose**;
> Preparation takes time and discipline and when you fight through the preparation time and you refuse to embrace it wholeheartedly, you extend the time;
> Whatever you are going through right now, is **building a character** within you; a character needed to **sustain your calling**;
> So, don't sweat the experience, surrender to it and learn so you can be promoted in due season;
> While your Creator has filled you with his gifts, **YOU MUST RECEIVE the gift**. Sadly, there are some of us who enjoy giving and are not great at receiving not even a simple compliment.

You should understand that people giving back to you is part of the divine order. His word states clearly: "Give and it shall be given back to you. Good measure, pressed down, shaken together and running over will men give unto you. And with the same measure you give, it shall be given unto you." Not wanting to be blessed by others simply violated the order of things and is a walk in disobedience~ something to think about the next time someone wants to bless you, be it financially or just a word of encouragement; if you have been a giver , just receive it and move on.

- ➤ As you **receive the dream or vision**, begin to seek further clarity with it. Ask yourself tough questions, what does the Creator want me to do?
- ➤ Consistently clarify the vision as our lives often are clouded with "stuff" that have the tendency to dilute the purity of our vision.
- ➤ As clarity develops, your brain is equally clear to build on what you have seen and what you believe to be your vision. Therefore, being to **quantify the vision**. In other words, what do I have that I need to bring to the table and what is the dream or vision going to cost? Keep your eyes on the starting gate, and your feet on the ground – Theodore Roosevelt.

Most divinely orchestrated ideas cost more than we have! So, just understand that! Most God-given ideas will stretch you and cause you to use the part of your brain that may often seek to lie dormant.

Many times, some of us just want others to bring things to the table while we sit back and just want to drive the boat. This is certainly the wrong approach to winning. And if you are one of those, I will urge you now to reconsider your ways. It doesn't matter how small it is, besides your vision you must always have something else to bring to the table. This is you investing in yourself and your vision. Often, we will not always get the chance to meet with the persons we admire. However, there are other avenues that allow you to glean from the expertise and wisdom of others. This is often by way of their books, CDs and anything they have presented to the public. This includes attending their conferences. If we are having problems even paying for that and we just want everything freely handed over to us; we are in a heap of trouble. How is a clenched hand to be blessed when it is totally closed. As you pour out to others,

others pour out to you. A closed hand will never be blessed. It will never have more than enough but will always operate within that which it contains. When you are unable to make sacrifices to even invest in your own vision; when you have difficulty even purchasing a ticket to attend a conference which can potentially take you off the *life support* into an extraordinary realm of possibilities, YOU ARE IN A HEAP OF TROUBLE!

> ➢ **Deliver the dream**. This is a poignant point which will warrant further explanations at a latter part of this journey.

Several months ago, my business partner and I met a young lady who is a pastor and a prophet. We were in the throes of formulating the Mission, Vision and Goals for our coaching company called Let's Go Innovate ™ (www.letsgoinnovate.com). We knew we'd been called to coaching God's children and teach them how to generate wealth for his glory. We were particularly tired of seeing women experience hardships especially those who were experiencing divorce and are now left behind to fend for their families; we were inundated with requests from women wanting to be mentored. In addition, we had gotten the spiritual auctioning to proceed. This young prophet visited us and posed a question: "Are You Ready?" She repeatedly asked that question until we began feeling concerned that perhaps in our excitement with starting a new venture and helping others to live their best lives, perhaps we were not getting the actual message. After several minutes of pondering on what she'd asked us, she went further to ask us what we believe Let's Go Innovate was. Of course, by this time; our mouths were moving way beyond our thoughts. We were confident in what we were sharing with her. Her response was "You are **a birthing or a delivery room where Thrones and Kings are born**".

Oh my! Quite a responsibility I thought to myself. This has become our slogan and the message we put ahead of us as a vision torch. It is the litmus test we use when opportunities come our way. It helps us to gauge if the opportunity aligns with our vision message and if it doesn't align, we are glad to let it go. Pastor Olivia Precious Cooper, the President of I Am Precious International nailed it in the head. Since accepting that word, our lives and Let's Go Innovate have changed. We continue to hear great testimonies of how God is pouring into his children, new vision, expanding vision, clarifying vision and launching visions. What an incredible ride!

When you **dare to deliver the dream** your Creator has bestowed upon you, even the atmosphere must align with that birth, if you **take action.**

Often people talk about magical events occurring around them; some call it prophesies being fulfilled and others call it MAGIC! Here is my thought on that, whatever you choose to call it, magic will only happen when preparedness meets opportunity. When these two ingredients collide in your life, you have no choice but to act! In addition, Magic is believing in yourself; if you can do that, you can make anything happen – Johann Wolfgang. The trouble however is if you don't take a risk, you stand the chance of losing more and giving more opportunity to failure. Many of us are so full of pride and fear. The truth be told, just like Cher said it: Until you are ready to look foolish, you'll never have the possibility of being great.

I urge you to take a break, and look in the mirror. If you don't have one at home, go get one! Now, talk to YOURSELF. Tell yourself about the good, the bad and the ugly… about your decision making strategies, in the past and present. Now, move to the future, remind yourself WHO YOU ARE (remember, you completed that exercise earlier). Pour into yourself while you take this journey. If you have been slack with your vision, ask important questions! WHY? And what have I done with my vision thus far? Out of hard questions, truth evolves and solutions germinate. Whatever answers you get from these questions, always remember that winners make goals, while losers make excuses – Unknown. This is no time for excuses. But time to truly encounter yourself and your reasons for ensuring your vision never hits the back burner again! I love Nike's quote, the only one who can tell you "you can't" is you. And you don't have to listen. It is a lie from the pit of hell. In other words, you are who you say "YOU ARE". You are what you say you see in the mirror. You are what you hear yourself say about YOU. If you are constantly calling yourself is tired old fool, well, that is just who you are. In you every own eyes, you will find yourself morphing into just that… *a tired old fool.*

➤ Often, we question our abilities and doubt if we were really called to do what is imprinted in our hearts to do… especially when a series of challenges seem to undermine our vision.

In these times, it is important to note that spiritual dreams, that is, divinely orchestrated visions are birthed through the process of divinely orchestrated delivery. Any woman who has birthed a child would understand this; that in delivery you are stretched to the max. You conserve your energy at the onset of the pregnancy and then exert it when the actual labor begins. Likewise, when you are birthing a divinely orchestrated vision, your mind is stretched, your heart extended and on the day ordained that you put this baby, that is your vision, to bed; you must push past your body, mind and push through the lies the enemy would whisper in your ears. As your delivery mid-wife called to help you push through your vision and this divinely designed adventure, your vision torch', I say to you... begin to push through now....Push through the sarcasm of people around you, those who have told you that you will never make it; push through the ones who are constantly putting stones and barriers ahead of your vision; push through your own mind which is constantly hounding you with untruths... telling you that you are not worthy of such great gift. PUSH THROUGH RIGHT NOW!

➢   One crucial nugget of wisdom is this... that you must be prepared for what is desired. It is one thing to want to have a husband, it is another to be prepared for the arrival of that man in your life. It is a great desire to want to bear children, it is another to be completely prepared for the baby's arrival. Likewise, wanting to be operating in the fullness of ones' vision or in ones' gifting will not make it happen. It is you taking action.... Consistent action that will yield results.

So, what have you most desired in your heart lately, and what are you doing to move that vision forward? Sadly, many of us want EVERYTHING BUT GIVE NOTHING! We want everyone to provide for us and sacrifice their lives and that of generations after them to US, yet we are not willing to sacrifice anything. We automatically presume that others do not need as much help as we do, so we expect them to be at our beck and call and not once do we take the time to even ask what the other person may need. Something is wrong with that mindset. The word of GOD says, **GIVE** AND **IT SHALL BE GIVEN TO YOU**....This denotes reciprocity. Here is my candid advice to us all, straight from my vault of wisdom; if your vision is way bigger than you can comprehend (which I suspect it will be, if it is divinely inspired), then start by giving what you desire the most to others. The most difficult hand to bless is a clenched fist.

When you hold your hands out, fully clenched, how are blessings expected to flow in your hands? As you begin to let go and open your palms and as you begin to share the very little you have with others, more will flow into your palms and pretty soon, it will be more than sufficient for your household and others.

➤ Here is a question for you: When was the last time you truly blessed someone? Yes, prayers are great but I am talking about being a real financial blessing? I am not asking for a reason why you couldn't do it… I am simply asking you what have you done for someone lately? BE CANDID. *You shall know the truth and the truth shall set you free* (John 8:32).

> Jot down what exactly did you do to bless that person?

> How did it make you feel afterwards to be a blessing?

> Would you do it again? Why or Why not?

➤ What would it mean to you, if someone took up your case as you did with others? Either actively or inactively? That is, if you have been ignoring the plight of others in your surroundings and have been focused on just you, how would it make you feel if someone did the same to you? On the other hand, if someone had quickly taken up your case just as you did others, what impact would that have made in your life? We make a living by what we get. We make a life by what we give – Winston Churchill

----

> ➤ How can you be better at responding to others' situations?

I can tell you how many times I have heard people say, when I become this… or when I become a millionaire, I will give to the poor and I will make the world a better place. While that is a noble thought, I submit to you that money will not draw out of you what you cannot sacrifice. The level of sacrifice is what builds integrity and great character! If we are not able to share the vey little we have now with others, when the money finally comes, there will always be other pertinent things which will challenge your initial thought and will eventually take up the place of the early promise you made. It is not when you have all the money in the world, that you will suddenly became charitable and if that is the case, then one would have to wonder if you were doing that to be seen and to receive the accolades of men or if you were truly doing that because you know it is the right thing to do. Many of the wealthy people we see today started giving when they had nothing. Because of their diligence in the little things, more was trusted unto them, so that now the world sees how much they do for others, not the other way around. The shortest way to reaching your own goal and accomplishing your vision is sowing into the lives of others. What we have, no matter how large or almost non-existent, we are not meant to hoard it. Hoarding is a disease which will ultimately take over other parts of our lives if we allow it to rule our decisions. Where your purse or wallet is, your heart follows. Humility is not thinking less of yourself. It is thinking of yourself less. If you focus on others, you forget you -Rick Warren. If you are therefore looking to open the doors of possibilities in your life, START GIVING! Happiness is not something you postpone for the future; it is something you design for the present- Jim Rohn.

MY LOVE LETTER TO FRIENDS & FAMILY after one of my journeys to AFRICA in 2011. Perhaps, you will learn one or two lessons from it:

"It is 1.50am TN time and I am still up because of jet lag. I have decided to take this time to simply thank God for family and friends, supporters and well-wishers who continue to support my effort in Africa. It is amazing how when we sacrifice to make others' dreams come true regardless of what we may be going through; when we truly and genuinely seek goodness for other people, great things happen in our lives too! These past weeks have been a roller coaster of life experiences for me. There are great testimonies from my recent trip to Nigeria; some of which I will be sharing soon...Bottom line, whatever your hand finds to do, PLEASE DO SINCERELY because YOU JUST DONT KNOW WHO MAY BE WATCHING... So help, not to get anything back but simply to lend your arms and legs to God.

Today, I am even more inspired to do more as God will have me…. What's in your hands today? What are you doing to make a change in someone else's life? Are you waiting to become a millionaire before you can change a life? Are you simply swallowed by life's ups and downs that you are not able to see through helping others? What you make happen for others, God will make happen for you. A great lesson that has manifested in my life these recent weeks! http://www.adassafoundation.org

PS: Enjoy the picture of the very first community library opened in

Emure Kingdom, Ekiti State and that region! Yeah God! This one is for you! I urge others to please join in making a difference in our children's' lives in Ekiti. They deserve the best because in my opinion, they are SIMPLY THE BEST. So when you give, do not give your left overs but your best...."

Courtesy of Princess Fumi & Adassa Adumori Foundation

Write down your take away lessons from this chapter:

_____

_____

_____

_____

No pain, no gain, really?

It's my pleasure to serve….

Experience teaches only the teachable.

Aldous Huxley

4 WHAT'S YOUR PLEASURE?

If you have ever felt insignificant in the course of your life; if you've ever felt like your contributions have not been recognized; if you've ever doubted that your gift or who you are matters to anyone, here is a wonderful chapter for you…. That's right, another wisdom nugget from my vault. As we journey through this chapter, here is a pivotal question I pose to you: Do you really believe that you get what you desire or pray for? In my 2RespectMyLife™ series (Check the eBook: My Destiny's Quill: Effective Life Strategies for Successful People: A DREAMER'S JOURNAL (RESPECT YOUR LIFE SERIES- Amazon), I discussed in details by providing a clear example of how a young girl called Rhoda in the bible shot from obscurity to walking in her destiny. I urge you to pick up the eBook as it is a great companion book to this one.

Faith is daring the soul to go beyond what the eyes can see – William Newton Clark. Faith is a strong ingredient to moving forward with our vision. Without faith, we will grow weary, and when we get weary, we will only be removed farther from our vision. It is therefore imperative that regardless of what our immediate circumstances dictate, we must push through with faith and trust that the vision is for an appointed time and that it will come to pass. WE MUST HOWEVER DO OUR OWN PART! That is, ONLY YOU CAN IGNITE YOUR VISION WITH THE TORCH! No man can do for you what you ought to do, but that which already lies half asleep in the dawning of your knowledge – Kahlil Gibran.

The knowledge you garner through the years, your belief system, YOU, as well as the Creator's PROMISES are the ingredients in your torch to light your vision and set it ablaze for the whole world to not only acknowledge, admire but partake of. All of these ingredients must exist for ignition to occur. Did you also know that you can be a tool to catapult your own vision to success or self-destruct? YOU are the only constant feature in the scheme of things....YOU have the power to move your vision forward or stagnate it. YOU are the only one who can steer it because it was uniquely designed for you. It has your DNA imprinted on it and if anyone else dare to steer it, they will self-destruct, unless you give it away. Armed with this knowledge, decide what you want, decide what you are willing to exchange for it. Establish your priorities and go to work – H.L. Hunt. No one promised you an easy ride neither did anyone say it won't require or stretch your imagination.

Often, our minds are all scrambled together like a jigsaw puzzle. It is at this juncture that it's important that we make every effort to offload the thoughts cluttering our minds and paining our hearts; those thoughts which ultimately cloud our judgment. Take a look at the following picture and write down what you see? Remember, beauty is in the eye of the beholder. The eye is the seat of the soul and what you see will ultimately dictate and chart the course of your vision.

Image courtesy of Jennifer Ellison at FreeDigitalPhotos.net

Now, write down what you see in this picture? How can you relate it to your current state of affairs? Can your description of what you see here be related to your current state of mind or the thoughts you have about your present circumstance(s)?

If what you have come up with has any negative connotations to it, how can you turn this around? What is your pleasure? That is, what you desire utmost in your heart must drive how you choose to tackle this question, so take your time with this question.

For you to ignite your dreams and harness your vision, you must have a clear understanding of where you want to go with this vision. Having the passion for one thing is just a step in the scheme of things that must occur to allow your vision to be birthed; although it is a great fuel to ignite the dream and harness the vision. Harnessing thus implies significant action on your part. I am yet to see anyone harness anything sitting down! A farmer in Africa goes to a farm to harvest some yam. In preparation, he makes a list of all the tools needed: his hoe, cutlasses, basket he would need to carry the yams away from the farm to the marketplace for sale as well as transportation to the market. Not only that, he goes further to bring along what he would need to replenish his own strength too as working hard on a heated summer day could dehydrate him! He leaves no stone unturned. He thinks of every areas he could fall short of ahead of time and tries to address those areas. He does this to make sure that when he is finally ready to harvest the yam, nothing stops him…. Not even himself! Above all, he ensures that he shows up at the right season for harvesting. This analogy is relevant to our harnessing our vision. Some of you have fragments of the ingredient needed to ignite your dreams or /and harness. Perhaps this is why many seem to be having difficulty manifesting their vision. Every component of the ingredients needed must be present. Some of these ingredients would take time to manifest while others will require pressure….massive pressure to birth them. But in the fullness of time, when all of the ingredients are in place, including the actions we must take on our part, MIRACLE HAPPENS! No one builds a house without first counting its cost. Likewise, every vision comes with a price tag, spiritually, emotionally, physically and yes, financially! If you are one of those who believes in getting everything for free without investing in your vision and dreams; let me be the one to tell you that you have just embarked on a strenuous road. Nothing in life is free! Your life was not free! It was paid for through the blood of the redeemer who hung on the cross! He paid a price, which was his life for yours and, if he did that, it means that your life, vision and life mission were valuable enough to justify a sacrifice. So why won't you sacrifice your "little change or coins" to ensure the fulfillment of your dream? If you don't like something, change it. If you can't change it, change your attitude – Maya Angelou. Either way, your vision is going to require a level of change inside out. If we are tired of the way we are living, we must be that change agent we are desperately looking for. Change will not come if we wait for some other person or some other time. We are the ones we've been waiting for. We are the change that we seek – Barack Obama.

Living and breathing our dreams and vision demand that we are ready to make whatever change is necessary in our lives, be it inwardly or in our environment to ensure the successful delivery of what we so desire. I love this wisdom nugget from Steve Jobs, "For the past 33 years, I have looked in the mirror every morning and asked myself 'If today were the last day of my life, would I want to do what I am about to do today?'" And whenever the answer has been 'No' for too many days in a row, I know I need to change something. Simple yet profound. No wonder when it was time for him to go, he provided a legacy that others are now following. Isn't it amazing that we often think of wanting to change the world, yet often we are unwilling to change ourselves? Show me a person who is bent on not changing and I will show you a person who is not really living life to its fullest. Often, we are afraid of changing our status quo because of the pain associated with change. However, to fulfill our vision, we must accept that discomforts, setbacks, challenges, and frustrations are often part of the whole journey. This mark of war you garner during the pruning season is what shapes your character, a character required to sustain you not only on your journey but also when you arrive at your destination.

Change, like sunshine, can be a friend, or a foe, a blessing or a curse, a dawn or a dusk – William Arthur Ward. So, I ask you again, what is your pleasure? Would you rather go through the painful part now, pass the test and move on to your destination or would you waste your precious moment fighting through life's difficult lessons? Either way, the lessons are going to come. It is now up to us how we adapt to those lessons.

(a) What are recent life lessons you learned in these areas? (b)What were your immediate responses to these life lessons? (c) What could you have done better? (d) And what is your way forward in each of these areas? If there is no struggle, there is no progress- Frederick Douglass. So, let's carry on with these exercises without holding back.

(1). Home front (Individual/ Family):

_____
_____
_____
_____
_____
_____
_____
_____
_____

(2) Emotionally:

_____
_____
_____
_____
_____
_____
_____
_____
_____

(3) Physically:

_____

_____

_____

_____

_____

_____

_____

_____

_____

_____

(4) Spiritually:

_____

_____

_____

_____

_____

_____

_____

_____

_____

_____

(5) Career wise:

_____

_____

_____

_____

_____

_____

_____

Other life lessons (if any):

The goal of this chapter is to help you begin to frame your thoughts around character building and the importance of "CHANGE" being an undeniable ingredient in achieving ones' life vision. Isn't it amazing that we are constantly looking for that magic wand, that magic bullet that will totally turn things around for us? Usually, when we are unwilling to do the work, unavoidable work will eventually push us in a direction we may not always like. YOU ARE THE MAGICAL BULLET YOU SEEK! Welcome to your life canvas where you get to write your story, inspired by your thoughts and emotions, fueled by YOU and YOU ALONE! Knowing this nugget of truth, it is therefore imperative that we are intentional with our decisions; intentional with the work we put into our lives and intentional about way forward on anything we choose to do. We can't be selfish; we can't be self-centered and we can't be greedy! Simply intentional. There is a difference. Francis Bacon put it ever so nicely, Things alter for the worse spontaneously, if they be not altered for the better designedly. Argh! It requires an Intentional decision making process. When we drive our decisions with intent, we have the capacity to dictate and / or predict the outcome. But if we leave things to chance, chances are the results we get will not be pleasant or to our liking. What is your pleasure as you read this? Are you getting the whole idea? A wise man once said, in order to succeed, your desire for success should be greater than your fear of failure ~ Bill Cosby.

Winston Churchill puts the whole concept in great perspective when he said success consists of going from failure to failure without loss of enthusiasm. So if you have had periods of great "failure" welcome aboard, you are now qualified and approved. If you have not had much failure, don't worry, you will acquire these life gifts. They are not meant to scare us but to "grow us". Life is not about being too careful but about living it to its fullness, within reason and within the will of our creator for us. A successful man is one who can lay a firm foundation with the bricks others have thrown at him ~ David Brinkley. So don't worry when people throw stones at you, they are only helping to qualify you quickly for the vision at hand. When Michael Jordan was asked the secret of his success, this is what he had to say… that he had failed over and over again in his life and that is why he can now say he has succeeded in more ways than one. Our goal is not to necessarily aim for success if that is what we desire but to simply do what we love and believe in and success will come naturally. A key to igniting your dream and harnessing your vision is this, striving to be a man or woman of value and substance. This will get you to success faster than constantly striving to be successful. Success is to be measured not so much by the position that one has reached in life as by the obstacles which they have overcome ~ Booker T Washington.

What then is the first step? **BE AWARE**. You cannot change what you are not aware of. If you are unable to assess your current situation truthfully, it will be impossible to change what you can't acknowledge. So, be aware of your current situation, how you got there, why you got there and the players in the adventure called 'your life". The second step is to be in **ACCEPTANCE.** How do you change what you can't accept? Denial is not only a great killer of dreams and vision; it is the seat of confusion and abject poverty. If everyone else is seeing your condition clearer than you are, there is a problem there. The truth does not change according to our ability to stomach it. ~ Flannery O'Connor. Part of being in acceptance of one's current status means acknowledging that whatever the circumstance is; it is temporary. We must take solace in the fact that as long as we work at it, it will become a thing of the past. I have never seen anyone steer a parked car nor seen a sailor steer a docked ship. Always bear in mind that your own resolution to succeed is more important than any other ~ Abraham Lincoln. If you can't find anyone to help steer your ship, steer it yourself! You will be better for it. If you fail to steer your own life boat, something else is waiting in the street corners to do just that for you. Your current circumstance is simply a mark of where the journey begins and not how it will end. Every action we take will either plant a seed of growth or otherwise in our lives. Now is the time to choose which seed we want to spend time growing in our lives?

What am I aware of today? (Explore candidly every areas of your life- physical, emotional, spiritual, and professional, other etc.)

What do I accept about this awareness?

What's Your Pleasure in this awareness and what is painful?

A while back, I was asked to be interviewed on a radio station in Nigeria, Africa. I thought really deeply about what I could share with the audience… what can make a difference in the lives of the people especially those who are striving so hard to make it in life… those who have been cheated… depressed…. Frustrated and often disappointed by life. How can we not only as a nation but as individuals move beyond reproach, depression, frustration, poverty and hunger? Is it possible to make anything out of one's life without money? In preparation, there were certain nuggets of truth which turned on some wisdom in my mind. It is my hope that as I share this with you here in summation of this chapter, a light bulb will switch on for you too.

As people who may have been through a lot of hardship, frustration and are desperately looking for solutions to better our lives; there is the tendency to believe that unless someone drops huge amounts of money on our laps, we will never make it. I am a sound witness that there are some of us who eventually find the money, yet happiness and success eludes us. Here is my belief and where faith is established, the favor of your Creator will take you where money cannot! The favor of God over your life will open doors in unusual places for you. It will cause you to dine amongst the elites in your society. God's favor and grace over your life will make the impossible possible for you. However, here is the catch … You are a great participant in this journey. Miracle happens when opportunity meets preparedness. All components of this major key that is Opportunity & Preparedness must be in existence for things to change in your life, which brings about a miracle. I titled the interview "Your Dream will take on Your Belief and Focus!"

Again, I was at lunch with one of my American Friends who has been around a lot of Africans. She asked me a poignant question…. She said to me: Why is it that Nigerians love to dabble in so many businesses at once? She was not saying it in a derogatory manner… she just needed to understand why almost all of the Nigerians she'd met, when she asks them what they do, they always ended up listing at least 3 or 4 different businesses. While I didn't have a great answer for her, it got me thinking about my own situation; all the types of jobs I have had in the US and also when I lived in Nigeria and concluded that many of us are dangling at the brink of our breakthroughs (without fully entering into them) because we simply lack focus and conviction about our DREAMs. If I were to knock at your door today, and I asked you what dream do you have, are you able to quantify it in one sentence, or will it involve several unrelated ideas? Please hear me, there is nothing wrong with having several businesses, but when you are starting out… it is important for you to stick with one simple vision. The English say, jack of all trade, master of nothing! What do you stand for today sisters and brothers? Just like Martin Luther King in the US had a dream to one day see his people free from prejudice and oppression, he was ready to pay a price for it because he knew his dream was larger than him.

What is your dream? Better yet, does your dream only involve you being rich or will it also bless others? More importantly, do you have enough faith to go after it, regardless of its cost? I want us to ponder on this… How many of us have dropped one dream for the other, hoping the new one will be the one to catapult us into great wealth?

Out of frustration, some of us have even gone to diabolical measures just to force things to happen for us. Know this, when we nurture self-centered dreams… when all we can see is how we have to survive… these types of dreams will not have longevity! So I urge you today… for you to overcome hardship, first examine your dream… ensure that it has a component to bless others. God's love binds us together and as we share the love for fellow human beings… as we become selfless, it is that love that will feed advancement into our lives.

Without God's Love, His Divine favor, and our love for each other, we will only find ourselves spinning around in circles. When you know God's love, that love will protect your dream from the enemy. It will allow your dreams to grow in an exponential way. Everything you need to make that seed you have been praying to grow is found in love. And as you create an environment of love, faith, divine favor and grace in your environment, you will see your dreams grow. Know this… contrary to common belief… money does not grow your dreams…. God's favor, His grace, your love for others, your commitment to your dream, and your relentless stride to ensure its fruition will cause your dream to come to pass. When you are aligned in this manner that I have described, your dreams will cause you to live your life at a different level… which is supernatural, more powerful than any diabolical source can oppose.

Back in the early 70s, Nigeria was different. People cared more for each other…. they helped each other achieve… they trusted more in each other. And if one person won, the whole neighborhood won! Today, sadly, Nigeria is not the same. We have the oppressed, the oppressors and those who just simply stay in between them to take advantage. Regardless, I still believe that there is hope! And this hope that I am talking about will only happen on an "individual" level. When each person learns to first appreciate who they are; appreciate life regardless of where they are; be grateful for little accomplishments, be thankful for whatever assistance we get from anyone as no one owes us nothing and more importantly, trust the author and the giver of life.

Another important key to fulfilling our destiny besides the power of focus is our BELIEF system. Do we have a belief system that will back up our dreams? The bigger your dream, the bigger the faith you need to push it out. The way we see our problems and challenges, will determine the result we get out of it. Persistence is a gift we must readily give ourselves… commitment to our cause is what we must exercise on a daily basis. If you allow doubts to step in, it will literally stop you from being what you are meant to be. Relentless faith on the other hand will also cause God's miracle to happen quickly in your life. Miracles happen in the atmosphere of love and peace. Many of us are very tired of running around because it seems there is no way… but I tell you this, that when you keep the right perspective about your situation… that this too shall pass… you will be amazed how events will change around you and will cause you to find favor in the least common places.

Here is a motto I live my life by on a daily basis… one which I have been talking about in a program called "Let's Go Innovate" a life and business coaching program developed by myself and my American partner, Yolanda Shields. When you believe, you conceive it, then you receive it. You will never get what you have not conceived in your heart and mind. Your faith will activate the miracle you have been looking for. Do you know that the person or the help you need may not necessarily come in the area of money but wisdom or other things? Don't under estimate the package God brings your way. Your miracle may not show up in the package you are expecting. So… be careful how you treat each other.

We must exercise the courage to be who we know we are called to be. It is time to shake off the self-pity and put on a new attitude… We are called to be a victor and not a victim! Equipped with this arsenal knowledge of who we really are, we must choose to quit blaming everyone and everything around us but look inwardly at ourselves, quit allowing life to overwhelm us but look boldly at our challenges and trust that it shall surely come to pass.

In tough times, have the right perspective… shake off the self-pity and be strengthened to succeed in life, regardless of whether you have money or not today. We often make right decisions when we allow our spirit to calm down. When you wake up in the morning, encourage yourself and remind your spirit man that you are a special creation… expect to have an amazing year … regardless of what the enemy says. Get ready to prosper and be a change maker in your community.

Delay is not denial. Thomas Edison, known for his creation of the incandescent light bulb said this that he did not fail 999 times, but just found 999 ways to NOT make a light bulb. This man was an inventor who tried to create a project and 999 times he tried. Today, we all benefit from that discovery. What if he had stopped at 10 when he got tired? What would have happened? Many of us, once we try something once or twice and there is no head way, we quickly jump ship and start something else.

This year, I urge you to choose to focus on one idea at a time. You get better at what you practice and work on. When you put more than one thing in your basket, you dilute the energy needed to push the right idea out. Think about this for a second. A position of peace is a position of power and when you are resting, your creator is at work making the crooked paths straight for you. So, I urge you today, as someone who has been through herself and have lived to enjoy success and victory, I urge you never … never…. never… to give up on your dreams regardless of how it looks… never give up on yourselves as there is a divine calling for each one of you… his precious gift to the universe.

Finally, I am of the opinion that there is a time for everything under the sun, the moon and the stars. A time for the wicked to reign and a time for their downfall, a time for the downtrodden to rise again… a time for the poor to be wealthy, be it in spirit, body, soul or financial wealth. Often, our background or upbringing appears to dictate what we choose to believe of ourselves. And quite frankly in Africa where there are so many diabolical forces going against each other, one may almost be resigned to the idea that one may never make it in life.

On the other hand, you have those who truly want to help yet those whom they have helped initially have come back to repay them in hatred, deceit and disappointment. The same people they reached out to help are the same people who want to crucify them. Many believe just one person will take care of the whole country. We must get it right somehow… "It takes a village to raise a child". When a whole nation reaches out to one person for assistance, how would you expect that person to fare?

Here is a lesson I have also learned through the years, while people want me to be everything and while my heart really wants to do more, "it really does takes a village to raise a child" One man or one woman cannot heal the entire crisis in a nation or a community. We all have our role to play whether we have money or not. So, here is a thought I want us all to consider… If we all wait for when we have money to do something in our community, we will wait forever. People automatically assume that just because one helps to impact a community it means one has money to save the world… This is absolutely false! Please allow me to use myself as an example, many of the things I was able to accomplish were not because I had extra money to throw around but it was a conscious decision that I made and the promise I made to God and myself that regardless of what… if I have to overlook my lunch, I will make a difference in the lives of my people. I also understand that I will not always be able to say yes to everyone. A hard lesson but one I needed to learn.

We must be reasonable in our thinking and our demands of others. This starts with our minds…. What do we occupy our minds with on a daily basis? Hatred or Love? As citizens of this world, we have some choices… to either let rage occupy our lives, bitterness towards others eat us alive, or we can get up and make things happen in our own lives. The Americans have a saying, that when life deals you lemons, you make lemonade. Do you know that even out of "nothing", great things can come? You may probably be having a hard time wrapping your mind around this…. Yes, out of nothing, something great can happen!

My final nugget of wisdom for you in this chapter is this and please, know this deep down in your heart… and deliberate on it on a daily basis…. All the forces of darkness cannot keep you away from your destiny… You are the only one that can and will present obstacles in your life… your thinking… your belief system, your faith or lack thereof will ultimately determine where you end up. No matter how many people told you , that you will never make it… no matter how many times they try to sabotage you or don't show up for what you do, do not let the decisions of a minority undermine that which you know of yourself. You must know and be utterly convinced that what is yours is yours and no one can take it away from you, not even the cynicism of people… their evil agenda around you. There is a season for everything; the time is here… the time is now and it begins with you! Harnessing your vision will require a new level of innovative action. Be prepared to take off the limits! Be determined to accelerate further and faster. You must invest in yourself by educating yourself and learning what others have done to be successful.

TAKE-AWAYS from this chapter:

--What differentiates those who make it from those who do not is not what others give them, it is their personal tenacity… their determination and commitment even when no one is there to give them money… they will still make it! --Blessings do not always come in monetary value, even though that is what many of us think… there are times God will plant someone in your life, just to encourage you… to keep pushing you forward with words of wisdom. Sadly, we often miss it because we have it in the back of our minds how people are supposed to be a blessing to us. Think back to your past… which angel has probably come your way and you have kicked out of your life because they have not come to you in the right package?

---Be kind to yourself and be kind to your fellow human beings
---Acknowledge and be grateful even with the little or "none" you think you may have;

---Value people around you, even when they don't come to you in the package you are expecting;

---Understand that no one owes you anything and you can always make lemonade out of the lemons you have;

---It takes a village to raise a child... so when someone reaches out to bless you, be grateful no matter how little they may do;

---What is in your hands, regardless of the size, you can use it to make something out of your life;

---Respecting and Valuing your elders will take you farther than what your mind can comprehend;

---Know this, whatever you are facing is temporary not permanent. Don't let people or circumstances get you upset. Don't let people undermine who you are... you and God are a majority... What looks like a stumbling block today will become that which will catapult your into your destiny. It doesn't matter what people around you do, it doesn't matter what government does or not, what God wants to do in your live is not dependent on what our government leaders do. They will have to answer to the divine creator.

--Take the limits off the divine creator and yourself. Accelerate your future and allow his divine power to overwhelm your lives today.

---In all of your ways, acknowledge God and He shall direct your paths.

Tenacity, Persistence and Commitment will take you, where mere DREAMS IN YOUR HEAD WILL NOT! If you don't have a dream, you don't have a direction...vice versa. Lessons Learned from my African friends and family Above all, don't go around saying the world owes you a living. The world owes you nothing. It was here first – Mark Twain.

Where are we going with this?

And What's Fire and Torch Got To Do With It?

The only true wisdom is knowing you know nothing.

Socrates

5 WILL SOMEONE PLEASE STOP THE HURRICANE?

Many times when we are in the throes of our life gifts; we desperately want the pain to stop. We are eager to move beyond the trials and gladly move on to the pleasurable times. It is times like this that we need to exercise caution; to ensure that we learn all we can learn from that experience before proceeding. We want the hurricane to move quickly out of the way, so we can begin to live our purpose and / or destiny. "*Watch Out world! Here I come!*" Our hearts pounding away and looking forward to unleashing ourselves on the world. If there is anything I have learned through my life experiences is that we are better off allowing the pruning however it comes, taking our time to be diligent with the lessons these experiences carry with them; so we don't self-destruct or destroy someone else's life while pushing our own agenda.

We give people less credit than we ought to. The truth is that people will smell fakeness from a mile away. Therefore, authenticity is crucial when in the valley of experience. As I stated in one of my conferences, the world is full of half-baked leaders who live a certain way in the dark and yet portray something different in broad daylight. We have leaders both in the secular, political and sadly in the religious circles demanding a certain way of living from others while their lives are fake as they could possibly be. How can you claim to be a pastor who cares for his sheep, yet when the time arises to show that true agape love, you don't? You will rather gauge with your physical eyes who that person is to you and what they mean to your ministry before even lifting your finger to acknowledge their presence? How can you be a political leader, when the only time the people see you do anything in the country or state or local government is when election is around the corner? How can you be a leader in an institution when all of your time is spent trying to figure out the next female body you want to exploit in exchange for good grades? How can you be a great leader when you are seen leading open demonstrations about different lifestyles yet you are the ring leader in your closet? How can you be a leader in your home when your life is in constant shambles and chaos and that is all your family sees?

Lord knows I have made many mistakes in my life and it is my desire that as I continue to gain the platform to share my life with people, others will be helped by them and make better choices. A man must be big enough to admit his mistakes, smart enough to profit from them, and strong enough to correct them ~ John C Maxwell. Now, this is loaded. Let's think about Maxwell's wisdom nugget for a second. Isn't it ironic that what we try to hide is actually the same gold mine we may have been looking for all of our lives? Because of pride, we often hide those things about our lives which are embedded in such richness in wisdom and even most times monetary value. Sharing our weaknesses and not just our strengths show others our vulnerability as well as our authenticity. By sharing our secret "faux pas" we let the world know that we are not perfect either and more importantly, we empower and encourage them to push forward as we have. We are only as sick as our secrets! We are often afraid of the repercussions of fessing up to the truth about ourselves; then end up living secret lives. A wise man is superior to any insults that can be put upon him, and the best reply to unseemly behavior is patience and moderation ~ Moliere. With the good times, equally roll in the bad times. It is all in perspective and our actions as they roll in. Whatever hurricane or wind which blows our way, we must first understand the importance of preparedness. After which we must equally accept that some events will happen that we do not have control over.

The pessimist complains about the wind; the optimist expects it to change; the realist adjusts the sails – Williams Arthur Ward.

Which one are you?

Whichever way you style your home is how others will perceive it. People will only see what you choose to expose to them. A fool flatters himself, a wise man flatters the fool – Edward G. Bulwer-Lytton. Many times, I have also observed people attempting to move a vision forward in the middle of chaos! While this is possible, this can be very tasking and draining. It is important that we maintain a sense of serenity around us if we want to move forward in our vision. It's not what you look at that matters, it's what you see – Henry David Thoreau. More often than not, chaos around us pushes us to see with an obscured mirror. In times of chaos, silence fuels the strength needed to birth our vision. Discipline is the bridge between goals and accomplishment ~ Jim Rohn.

What hurricane experiences are you facing in your life now? Don't be afraid to write them all out. My journal (eBook) in the RESPECT YOUR LIFE SERIES, *My Destiny's Quill: Effective Life strategies for Successful People DREAMER's JOURNAL* (Purchase on Amazon) is a great compliment on your journey to harnessing your vision.

What are your thoughts on how you ended up with these hurricane experiences? (Please note that we are not digging into the past here; we are simply assessing what may be the current obstruction to our achieving our dreams and walking majestically in our vision). Knowing the root of your problem is truly half the battle won! This is what we are doing here. So take your time, be true to yourself, acknowledge your present situation and let's tackle them one at a time using the tools here.

As stated earlier delivery requires strength and an incredible amount of PUSH on the side of the person carrying the baby. Imagine you are having a baby and, after twenty-four hours, you are still in labor. The physician comes in and tells you your baby is in severe distress and that they found that the cord is wound around the baby's neck! With every passing minute, the potential danger has moved into the realm of reality! The physician and nurses run around and they eventually wheel you into the operating theatre for a C-section. What just happened here? They were prepared for emergencies; they took action quickly because they had studied and had enough experience to know that they had to quickly do a C-section. Armed with all of these wisdom and knowledge, they proceeded and succeeded in helping you birth a healthy 8 lb. boy. This story truly happened and I was the one it happened to. Now, when it was time to have my second baby, I was more prepared. I knew my history of never dilating beyond 1 cm in 18 hours; the physicians had enough information to provide a genuine recommendation of C-section. I went for it without any fear. Because of my earlier experience, even though C-section was a painful process; it was more painful to stay in labor for over eighteen hours; then still have to do the C-section. I knew that was the best choice for me; so I took it. Thankfully my boys are both grown men now, living their best lives.

Now, come with me and think a little deeper, you will see that the above analogy mirrors us birthing our own vision. Often, we want an easy route or when we sense or perhaps was told what we were supposed to be doing in life; we don't anticipate hiccups. The chord suddenly wrapping around the baby in the womb is a hiccup within the delivery of your vision. The physicians and nurses around you in time of delivery are the ones ordained and assigned to help you birth your vision. Many of them will go ahead of you to help make the crooked paths straight; some will sit on the fence and man the fence to warn when there is a dangerous force attempting to abort the vision; and others will work alongside you to ensure a successful delivery. This tells me that a divine vision almost always involve others up-guarding you and helping you to push your success out. If you have been sitting and dining with people who are not meant to be a part of the vision, you may want to start assessing your circle of influence. This is another topic I am choosing to tailor in another book. The C-section is the tool needed to open the womb and bring the baby out. Life challenges will often come our way but it is the tools we garner during trials that help us when we are ready to push through. Don't knock the experiences you have had; they are marks of excellence and life's experiences which can be ultimately used to catapult you into your destiny.

A Hurricane is defined as a storm with a violent wind, in particular a tropical cyclone in the Caribbean. There are no other storms like hurricane on earth (aoml.noaa.gov). It is incredible the amount of damage that a hurricane can create on a nation or an individual. When used to describe a person, it could very well be interpreted as someone who I call a "fire cracker". That is, a bubbly, go-getter who does not allow anything or anyone to get in the way of his or her success. One who believes in what he or she is doing and making every effort to ensure showing excellence in all he or she does. In other words, as a firecracker of a person, you are on fire to make history; you are full of wisdom and compassion yet firm in most decision making.

How would you describe yourself? Be honest with yourself. There is no wrong or right answer, only an authentic one which will point you to your destiny.

How would you describe YOU before reading this book?

How would you describe YOU NOW that you have partaken of these wisdom nuggets called "Your Vision Torch"?

What change(s) do you foresee happening as a result of all of the thought provoking exercises you have done in this book?

How do you intend to make these changes? That is, write down your action plan here. Hope is a waking dream – Aristotle. Now, begin to steer and wake your dream up right here. It begins with you looking within to fish out the changes necessary and extremely vital to you harnessing your destiny. If you are not ready to look inside of yourself and you are not ready to truly dig in to uncover what has been the barrier to your success; then you are not ready to

LIVE A LIFE OF SUCCESS! Remember that your present circumstances do not determine where you can go; they merely determine where you start – Nido Qubein. Let that be an encouragement to you today as you dig way down for answers. Getting to the next level always requires ending something, leaving it behind, and moving on. Growth itself demands that we move on. Without the ability to end things, people stay stuck, never becoming who they are meant to be, never accomplishing all that their talents and abilities should afford them. Necessary Ending - *Henry Cloud.* As you dig further into the truths embodied in your disappointments and challenges, you will experience freedom... freedom to tell your own truth without fearing what others would think of you... freedom to know that you know... that you know who you truly are... freedom to just BE!

Lighting a fire requires a source. That is, without putting the torch in contact with a source of fire, no flames will occur. Your torch which is your vision needs a source of ignition. Many of us know the implication that has on our spirituality and the importance of our connection with "the source"…. The one who paved a way for the Israelites in times of need at the red sea (Exodus 14-15). It is important that as we look at our Vision, we also understand the importance of being spiritually grounded to ensure success which cannot be aborted. Sadly, many of us have been wounded by life experiences inside and outside of church gatherings that we have essentially given up on closeness with our Creator. I recently had some life changing experience with some pastors, those whom I had respected and thought they were true reflection of Christ. In recent times, they had disappointed me with their behaviors... the way they lived in the presence of others and what they really doing behind closed doors. I was truly disappointed and taken back with their unruly behaviors... behaviors which could really send a new covert right out of the church and into the devil's playpen. In the midst of these painful experiences, I also come to find my centeredness with the Creator. I have since learned and understood that my spirituality is not dependent on what a pastor or a spiritual leader does or not do. They will face judgment themselves so I don't have to judge them here. It is solely my responsibility to stay grounded and be in oneness with my Creator. I am learning on a daily basis to fix my eyes above and not on our leaders… to understand that they are also human beings who are subject to errors. But to also stand firm and ensure that my spirit is not killed by their callous and nonchalant behaviors. I have garnered that only I can make a change. And if the distraction is too much, simply remove myself from the situation!

Staying grounded in the source which ignites your vision is crucial to your success. The bible tells us that we were created in God's likeness (Genesis). We possess every virtue possessed by our creator. We have the power and the ability to ignite our world for good or evil. Likewise, we have the ability and the know how to ignite our passion and harness our vision. And because we were created in His image, we are the source we have been looking for all of our lives. That is, the fire to ignite our dream and harness our vision has been sitting right inside of us all along. The difference now is that as a vision delivery midwife, my role is to help you deliver this baby safely and without any complications. This is what the Vision Torch is intended to do for you.

For many of us, we have been carrying this baby for so long. Our backs are bruised, bodies essentially on fire with relentless pain; hearts throbbing uncontrollably; eyes deeming into spiritual blindness; ears clogged with the resounding clicks of sounds pouring out of our past failures. Many have even forgotten what they were created for because they are constantly overwhelmed by life challenges. For many, if delivery does not happen right now, they are more than likely to die... I mean physical death. Today, all we need look at around us to see are scores of people committing suicide out of desperation. A very good friend and sister attended a conference recently. She came back with a phrase which has truly been a blessing. Midwives come at the birthing moment -T.D Jakes. Get ready to birth destiny as you proceed with me on this journey...In fact, I do believe at this point many are beginning to birth their destinies. Taking a walk of faith as well as examining one's life, what could be a potential barrier and what strengths one possess to take back ones' vision is crucial to the manifestation of that which we desire.

If you are trying to achieve, there will be roadblocks. I've had them; everybody has had them. But obstacles don't have to stop you. If you run into a wall, don't turn around and give up. Figure out how to climb it, go through it, or work around it. _ Michael Jordan.

.

Igniting Ones Dream is Never Easy!

Wisdom Begins in Wonder.

Honesty is the first chapter in the book of wisdom.

Thomas Jefferson

6 LET THE GOOD TIMES ROLL!

Often when we have an idea; we are so elated at the thought of making that idea become a reality. In our hearts, we believe it is truly THE ONE that will eventually give us the financial means and know how to just be whom we are meant to be! Bravo! If you have an idea of creating or developing a product or service, I commend you. However, get this having the worlds' best idea will do you no good unless you act on it. People who want milk shouldn't sit on a stool in the middle of a field in hopes that a cow will back up to them – Curtis Grant.

Sometime ago, a girlfriend reached out to me about starting her own business. She was so excited that this particular idea was dropped into her spirit. I asked her how ready she was and she screamed through the phone "I am so ready and so done with the corporate world. I know I need to be doing my own thing rather than giving my knowledge away for free!" Well, needless to say I jumped on her band wagon and became her cheerleader. Few weeks later, I checked in with her to find out how far she'd gone with her plan. In return, all I got was her static about all of the reasons why she could not start with her plan. "One thing or the other keeps getting in the way. The devil is a liar and I won't be stopped!" Needless to say, it took everything in me to yell out to her and tell her, at this juncture, if she could not find a more acceptable reason, she is probably the devil in her own way! Let us train our minds to desire what the situation demands. – Marcus Annaeus Seneca.

Starting a new business, developing a new product, creating a new brand, promotion within your work place, becoming a bestselling author, a celebrated artist or whatever you might throw in the mix; they all take effort and tremendous effort at making them happen. When you see someone on the news or anywhere and this person is someone you adore and wished you could be like, ask yourself this question "am I willing to pay the price?"
Once we accept the responsibility for our own actions; once we understand that we will have to push harder to find our purpose, once we make the commitment and decide regardless of what obstacles come our way; then ladies and gents I dare to tell you that may the good times roll. Your passion for your mission will ignite your vision. No vision ever became a reality without putting a footwork to it.

So for today, let's take this process a little deeper.
Have you been procrastinating about your vision or dream?
Write the lies you tell yourself about your vision or dream

right here. For example, I don't have enough money to start my business.

How do you perceive yourself as overcoming this procrastination? That is, what steps are you committed to taking to drop the procrastination and grab a hold of your dream once again? Remember, igniting your dreams will require a state of mind marked by abstraction and void of distraction.

Here we go, TODAY, I WILL…..(fill in the gap)

TOMORROW, I WILL ......

While this is a great starting point, get a notebook and begin to map this out on a weekly basis. And at the end of each day, I need you to come back to it and ask yourself the following hard questions:

What did I do today to push forward? Did I follow the plan written down? If you did Bravo! You are learning to be a person of your own words and someone who follows through regardless. If you have not done any of what you wrote that, take heart. Push harder. Ask this question and write down your answers, why didn't I follow through on

the plans I wrote down?
Write down what you know are simply excuses:

Write down what you feel are legitimate reasons:

What can I do tomorrow to ensure that I follow through?

Examine your heart and soul, what do you believe you have (i.e. qualities) to make your dream come alive? Remember the purpose of this chapter is to discuss and find ways to ignite your dream. The great thing about this section is that it allows you to come up with solutions which are feasible and only be carved out for you. Often, when we come up with solutions ourselves, we are inclined to see them through more so than when someone else tells you what you should be doing. Life happens at the level of events, not words – Alfred Adler

We live in a world where many are so dissatisfied with their current situation, yet sadly, very few want to do anything about it. Only you alone can ignite your dreams. You carry the torch of your vision and no one can envision what you have come up with. Others are only able to see your vision through your very own eyes and the enthusiasm you bring to it. If you are nonchalant with your vision, others will be too. No one should ever want more than you want for yourself. The only measure of what you believe is what you do. If you want to know what people believe; don't read what they wrote; don't ask them what they believe; just observe what they do – Ashley Montagu.

If you put three to six of your friends and family members in a room and I ask them what they perceive about you… regarding your personal life as well as your aspirations, hopes for the future; what do you think these people will say about you? Be honest, be real…. Remember authenticity is the building block to success. No one is perfect, so I expect at least one "not so great" commentary. It may even be what they perceive as a weakness in you. For me, it has always been allowing people to take advantage of me; giving my very last shirt to a person and having the person turn around to otherwise ignore my efforts. For years, I dealt with the pain of constantly letting go of friends who choose to be self-centered and hurtful. Today, I relish the ability to understand my friendship and alliances. I am able to discern who belongs in the CORE and who doesn't. And for those who do not, I appreciate their nuances as well as understand they are thorns which continually grow me. When we learn to accept people for who they are and recognize what role they are to be playing or not to be playing in your life; life becomes a little less complicated. For the good times to roll beyond your wildest expectations, take the time to gauge your friendship and alliances. Rearrange if need be. Bump up or down those you know serve no purpose because they are extra luggage bags which you will ultimately pay for to claim them.

For you to continue to glow in victory, with your dreams well ignited; you must work on enjoying the process on a daily basis, regardless of the challenges which may pour into your sacred space. Someone once said, that the door of opportunity won't open unless you, do some pushing - Anonymous. Are you ready to push and push real hard? Are you ready to let the good times roll? Remember, this will require some action on your part. The man who has done nothing but wait for his ship to come in has already missed the boat – Anonymous. We are called to do our own part and then leave the rest to the creator to conclude. One adage I always use to steer my vision is this, a parked car can only become useful when it is moving. If you park your vision or your dreams, it doesn't matter how many times you return back to the parking lot; it really doesn't matter how much of prayers and dancing you do around that parked car; IT WILL REMAIN PARKED unless of course if you believe in magic where things are extraordinarily transported. Life only demands from you the strength you possess – Dag Hammarskjold.

If you include any responses which may be construed as negative, why do you think that certain person(s) would say that about you?

In my lifetime, I have seen people who have been driven to become complacent due to their past experiences. Fear has taken literally over their lives and is not looking to plunge into any more experiences. While life experiences will cause us to be more in touch with our own feelings and often cause us to be more cautious with decisions we make; it is important that we not allow it to become a crutch to laziness or complacency. It is also important that we not allow it to fester too long that it becomes fear of failure to launch. With the raging storm comes, there is really nothing we can do but to ride the wave and trust that it will subside. Within us all there are wells of thought and dynamos of energy which are not suspected until emergencies arise. Then oftentimes we find that it is comparatively simple to doubt or triple our former capacities and to amaze ourselves by the results achieved. – Thomas J. Watson.

Often what keeps me going is knowing that the storms which come my way; if I stood still enough, there will be a bridge which will surface; a bridge to my life purpose one which will help me fulfill my destiny. It is wonderful when at the end of one's stormy season, beauty evolves. Trouble creates a capacity to handle it – Oliver Wendell Holmes, Jr. Your creator will never give you more than you can handle. When you relax and just let things be, trusting that all things will work for your good; you will be amazed how much clarity you will end up having in situations which you already question or are uncertain of. What God expects us to attempt, He also enables us to achieve – Stephen Olford.

What lessons do I want you to get out of this chapter?
(1). After the storm comes peace like a river;

Image courtesy of Photokanok at FreeDigitalPhotos.net

(2). There will always be beauty out of a raging storm for those who dare to dream yet again;

Image courtesy of Christian Meyn at FreeDigitalPhotos.net

Image courtesy of Julie A Wenskoski at FreeDigitalPhotos.net

(3) You must debunk the lies you tell yourself, the ones others tell you about yourself and the one's life experiences automatically download into your being on a daily basis, in order to move into your divinely orchestrated position.

Having said these, now let's quickly go over some thoughts here:
What is the **TRUTH** as I see it about my current situation versus **what the TRUTH as I tell it to myself and others**? Is there any disparity in both?

Again, what is **MY TRUTH** TODAY?

Again, what is **MY BIG LIE** TODAY?

Brave Souls Share their Stories

What is Your Story and Your "What if Story" Everyone's got One! Find Yours and You've Just Got a Breakthrough!

In the darkest hour, the soul is replenished and given strength to continue and endure.

Heart Warrior Chosa

7 ALL WORK AND NO PLAY

Now let's continue to put feet to all of the work you have been doing since the beginning of this adventure. First, if you are reading this chapter; I want to commend you for holding on and pushing through to get here. It is my hope that by now, you have not only gleaned some valuable knowledge, but garnered some wisdom and tools to help you push forward towards harnessing your visions and making your dreams come true. For your tenacity, you are absolutely on your way to success. Unveiling what have been the problems or stumbling blocks to your success is one step but taking action to make things happen and to change situations in your life is a step and indeed a necessary one towards your goals. So, get ready for life changing experiences as you plunge into developing daily strategies to acquiring your dream. Accept that all of us can be hurt, that all of us can —and surely will at times – fail.

Other vulnerabilities, like being embarrassed or risking love, can be terrifying, too.

Here are some wisdom nuggets I need you to digest while you deliberate and work on how to steer your vision and dream:

(1). Remember now, it is one thing to have an idea, it is another to steer it. This is what truly separates the successful people from those who are just talkers and not doers. ***Your dream or vision will not steer itself. YOU HAVE TO PUT FEET TO IT FOR IT TO MANIFEST.*** People are always blaming their circumstances for what they are. The people who get on this world are they who get up and look for circumstances they want, and, if they can't find them, they make them. - George Bernard Shaw.

(2). Here is another thought, ***brave souls stand up and be counted. You cannot allow your circumstances to cast a dark and evil shadow on your future.*** Those who sit down on their destinies…. Die without fulfilling any of it. A very famous adage I hear a lot which always steers me to action is this, that the grave yard is filled with books never written, plays never written, films never produced, businesses which never manifested and dreams which never surfaced. It wasn't that God was unkind to these people, it was simply that if they were able to be polled today; I bet many will tell us, I wished I had gotten up and at least put myself in the position to receive these gifts. We must learn to steer our vision and not wait for others to do this for us. It is our relation to circumstances that determine their influence over us. The same wind that carries one vessel into port may blow another off shore. – Christian Bovee. What didn't kill you, can't destroy you now.

(3). ***Only YOU have the capacity and the ability to sabotage yourself.*** We must realize this: We either make ourselves miserable or make ourselves strong. The amount of work is the same.-Carlos Castaneda. Having said that, choose your poison wisely. It is therefore very important that we create and use our circumstances to push us to the level we desire for our lives. Often, our circumstances are platforms for our life changing experience. So, if you are in a place where you are just simple confused about what you are supposed to be doing; if you are just absolutely bombed out of your mind and really do not know what the next step for you is... ask these questions:

(a) What ails you right now? That is, what are you going through right now that you believe it's totally unacceptable? What circumstances are keeping you up every night?

(b) What boils your spirit that makes you ask: there has to be a better way than this? What surrounds your life right now that you are so angry about and wished the circumstances could just turn around?

When you are able to truthfully answer these questions, there are usually nuggets of your destiny tied to them. You will only succeed in what you are passionate about. Heaven and hell is right now…. You make it heaven or you make it hell by your actions. – George Harrison.

If you find yourself in a situation you desperately want to quit, then make it happen! Circumstances will always remain if we do not get up and steer them. Only you are responsible for your own life! So quit expecting someone else to dictate your future. Don't get me wrong here, there are others your Creator will bring to your paths to help steer your dream but you can't force it…Those who God has called to bless you, you won't need to chase them down. Often, we target certain people because of what we know of them but we have to always realize that they can only do so much for everyone. They are human beings who need help too! If you reach out to people and they can't help, just move on and understand that your helper is on the way. Quit chasing people down, face heaven, take action and let HIM (God) work it all out for you. BUT YOU MUST TAKE ACTION! Your vision torch is in your hands right now and only you get to carry it to the finish line. You are the handicap you must face. You are the one who must choose your place. – James Lane Allen. Your vision will entail you taking up the torch and placing yourself in a place where opportunities can run after you. If you want to be found, stand where the seeker seeks. – Sidney Lanier. Hiding will not get you anywhere; neither will isolation bring to you what you desire. We are wired and design to connect with others and life cannot be lived in isolation. Don't hound or hunt people down, but place yourself in the path of opportunities, do your best to present YOU in an acceptable way and success will follow.

(4). ***Don't be obnoxious but be inquisitive about everything!*** It is when you consistently ask "why?" and "what if?" questions and develop "what if" scenarios.... Where all of these converge is often where innovation happens. Let's take little children as examples. They are very inquisitive, always asking daddy why this... mummy, why that... As they begin to ask more questions, they begin to grow in knowledge and wisdom. They are the purest of us all and they take life as they see it. Is nothing every straight in life ever straight and clear, the way children see it? – Rosie Thomas. You can't grow in what you don't practice.

(a) Create a "what if" and "why" story surrounding the vision for your life right now? (Please do not move past this section until you have completed this exercise. If you don't have time, please stop right now and wait till you have time to complete it.) Champions take responsibility. When the ball is coming over the net, you can be sure I want the ball. – Billie Jean King.

Do you know that success is simpler than we imagine?
Often we muddle up the waters with our own confusion
and acceleration of our inadequacies that we fail to see what
may be simply standing in front of us.

(5). ***Simplicity is essential to creating a successful path
to victorious living***. Keep things simple by learning to
eliminate the non-essentials things in your life. The ability
to simplify means to eliminate the unnecessary so that the
necessary may speak. – Hans Hofmann. This is very vital to
ensuring that our vision is manifested. Hence, to launch the
process of being, simply have fun generating your ideas. In
other words, do not make a chore out of creating a path for
your vision and dream to blossom. There is a master key to
success with which no man can fail. Its name is simplicity…
reducing to the simplest possible terms every problem. –
Henri Deterding.

Write down the many ways you can make life a little easier for yourself today:

HOME FRONT (family and self):

CAREER WISE & / OR BUSINESS:

RELATIONSHIPS (acquaintances, close friends, associates etc.)

Is this Truth or is this Dare?
Believe It! See it! Conceive it! Be Bold to Receive It!
What do you think about the phrase?

Can you apply the phrase to your life? If so, How?

If not, why not?

Rate your pulse. What are your thoughts on how to push forward with your vision? Remember, this is your story and nobody else's'. Here is where I want you to write how you perceive your life after all of the work you've done alongside this author in this book. Has any thoughts changed? If so, share what has changed in the way you feel you can approach life now? If not? Why not? (There is no wrong answer!).

Now that you have written your story...hopefully a new perspective to viewing your "life story," I want you to join me in looking at simple innovative steps towards igniting your dreams and harnessing your vision.

Here we go:

(1). *Have a Dream.*

This looks very simple but the truth be told, while some will tell you that they are doing some jobs because they need to put food on the table, many will tell you that they just don't know! Others will say they are just too confused to figure it out. It is therefore important that we have a dream. It is only when you have a dream that you will deliberately start looking for opportunities around you. How do you move forward when you have no direction as to where you are going? A new day is a new dawn and a second chance to make things right. And remaining open to unforeseen opportunities are simply God's gift to His children. Today a new sun rises for me; everything lives, everything is animated, everything seems to speak to me of my passion, everything invites me to cherish it. – Anne De Lenclose. An easy way to discover ones' passion, vision, mission or goal in life is to pay close attention to your surroundings. You will be surprised to truly hear a soft whisper ushering you towards your destiny. Learn what you are and be such. – Pindar.

(2). There is strength in Collaboration.

Have you ever heard of the adage, no man is an island? Well, it is true. It is important that we surround ourselves with people who will not only inspire us to be the best, but motivate, support, encourage and even chastise us when needed. When the student is ready, the teacher appears. When famous multimillionaire was asked about the secret to his success; he said this: that he has taken a long and hard look at his life; he understands his weaknesses and knows his strengths. He has learned to embrace them and look for others who have what he does not have. While many will attribute his success to his hard work, he attributes it to surrounding himself with powerful men and women who compliment him. Even when you are successful, your company will never go bigger than you unless you start trusting others and allowing them to fill in the empty spaces for you. And sometimes, it is not about working hard but working smart. The art of collaboration fosters smartness. Trouble shared is trouble halfed. – Dorothy Sayers. Therefore, it is essential that you establish your strategic alignment from the get-go. Your circle of influence is very pivotal to your success. Do you know that there are dream breakers and dream makers in all of our lives? While I will only be touching on this topic briefly in this book, please be on the lookout for a well detailed book on this topic at a store near you. Or better yet, keep checking my website: www.worldoffumihancock.com on a regular basis for updates. It promises to be a great read and an eye opener.

In the meantime, take a look at the following drawing and

jot down what comes to you. Though you may be tempted to brush past this picture, I urge you not to do so. Do not move past this it until you have answered the questions posed.

Your *Circle of Influence*
(How Deep and How Wide?)

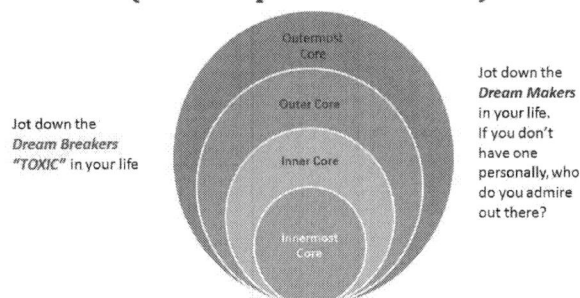

Jot down the
Dream Breakers
"TOXIC" in your life

Jot down the
Dream Makers
in your life.
If you don't
have one
personally, who
do you admire
out there?

Tell the truth, who has been occupying your innermost core?
A *Dream Breaker* or a *Dream Maker*
And you thought your best friend belonged in your innermost court.
Argh!

© Copyright 2013 Fumi Hancock

Jot down the **Dream Breakers,** that is, those whom you perceive as the **TOXIC** people in your life, but first define what you a Dream Breaker is? (This may be a list you really want to keep to yourself. It is simply an exercise to help you get rid of the load you've been carrying; loads which have often kept you bound to failure and lack of progress.

Why do you regard them as **Dream Breakers**?

Jot down who the **Dream Makers** are in your life:

Why do you regard them as **Dream Makers**?

Study the circle of influence and begin placing your
relationships into these circles. You must take care to be
very thoughtful when doing this assignment. What often
happens is that you find some of your current friends in a
circle you never imagined them to be in. If you have a
friend who you seem to believe you are always the one
doing for him or her and she /he never reaching out;
perhaps he/she does not belong in the circle you placed
them in the first place. These circles help us to understand
the types of friendships around us. It gives us the
permission we need to ensure we are not spending time
with time wasters; we appreciate those who are closest to us
and even those who are not. We accept people for who they
are and are not easily disturbed when they are simply being
what they are meant to be in our lives.

(3). Be the change maker and the leader you are looking for.
We are eagerly looking around for this image we have in
our heads of an authentic leader who will take us out of our
misery. We are called to be leaders ourselves. It starts with
us taking charge of our own situations; accepting
responsibility and making a determination to overcome
whatever obstacles which may be thrown my way. Nothing

can stop the man with the right mental attitude from achieving his goal; nothing on earth can help the man with the wrong mental attitude – Thomas Jefferson.

The Cardinal Rules for Igniting Your Dreams and Harnessing Your Vision are as follows:

Overcoming Your Challenges in Strides
To exist is to change, to change is to mature, to mature is to go on creating oneself endlessly. – Henri Bergson. Challenges only point us to our mission and vision in life, provided we allow it to. My great concern is not whether you have failed, but whether you are content with your failure – Abraham Lincoln.

How do you overcome challenges?

- *Believe and accept that change is growth.*
  To improve is to change; to be perfect is to change often. –Winston Churchill.
- *Step out of your comfort zone.*
  If there is no struggle, there is no progress. – Frederick Douglass.
- *Take the first step.*
  Faith is taking the first step even when you font see the whole staircase. – Martin Luther King, Jr.
- *Create and maintain momentum.*
  Don't dwell on what went wrong. Instead, focus on what to do next. Spend your energies on moving forward toward finding the answer. – Denis Whitley.

- *Face obstacles straight-ahead.*
  Do not fear mistakes. You will know failure. Continue to reach out. –Benjamin Franklin.
- *Focus on your objectives.*
  Learn from yesterday, live for today, hope for tomorrow. The important thing is not to stop questioning. - Albert Einstein.
- *Partner with development and potential.*
  I hope to stand firm enough to not go backward, and yet not go forward fast enough to wreck the country's cause. – Abraham Lincoln
- *Make change by seeking positive influence.*
  Your attitude, not your aptitude, will develop your altitude- Zig Ziglar.

Your Success Will Rely on You Taking the Necessary Steps to Succeed.

Stepping Out is Crucial to Harnessing Ones' Destiny!

Fail small to SUCCEED BIG.

Vadim Kotelnikov

8 THE WINNERS' CIRCLE …

January 2013, my life as I knew it changed incredibly for the better. It was barely two months after my very first Young Adult Fantasy Novel: The Adventures of Jewel Cardwell became a bestseller! That in itself, was a huge miracle. I had worked so hard for years, trying to not only make ends meet for my family but to also pursue my dream in the entertainment industry. Regardless of how competitive the arena was, I was ready to give it my all to make it happen. It was right after my virtual tour that people began to reach out to me, asking more of my African royalty background. In the midst of being inundated with ideas, my ah! ah! moment emerged. In addition, I was way more into finding innovative ways to re-invent myself and my career in the entertainment industry. What if I created a show online where I not only parody some funny celebrities who do funny things and then use the platform to promote my lifestyle talk show? Initially, I had a fear of not succeeding if I tried but it was soon overshadowed by letters and emails from people congratulating me on the young adult novel. In addition, they mentioned how one of the stories written about my background as an African Princess and my philanthropic work in African touched their hearts. They wanted to know more about me. Hence, it was the beginning of a journey which would literally change my life.

Innovation always starts with a question. It is not possible to create a great product or services without genuinely asking some hard questions. You will come to know that what appears today to be a sacrifice will prove to be the greatest investment that you will ever make. - Gorden .B. Hinkley.

After a much needed rest from my back to back virtual tour; an idea came was born~ to create an innovative lifestyle online talk where The Princess of Suburbia, my personae will be featured tackling everyday issues from health, to entertainment, relationships, love, life and everything in between. Six months into the show, the number of viewings bean to increase astronomically! By the eight month, I had garnered to myself well over 2.25 million viewings! And a host of other personalities interested in sharing the sit with me. Since its launch, I have completed yet again another book, a business book which you are now reading; started a coaching company with a friend, Let's Go Innovate which we regard as the birthing room for visions and dreams; was invited to grace the red carpet at the African Oscars alongside a Nollywood Producer who eventually won the award in her category; was invited by the

President of African Oscars to endorse the event; wrote an original screenplay which is being produced and directed in Nashville TN, my very first feature film showcasing my Alta ego, The Princess of Suburbia ™ of the Princess in Suburbia TV Show (Enjoy some of my episodes at: www.youtube.com/user/princessinsuburbia). Great minds discuss ideas; average minds discuss events; small minds discuss people. Eleanor Roosevelt.

If there is anything I have learnt in this journey, is the importance of truly steering our gifting's. We cannot continue to live in complacency and waiting for a magical circumstance to occur in our lives. We must take charge of our vision and not only be in tune with it, but be extremely committed to making it happen. There are so many things in the world which can dissuade us from moving forward with our dreams. But our dedication to it, will be the driving force to catapult us to the next level. The future belongs to those who believe in the beauty of their dreams – Eleanor Roosevelt.

I often asked myself this question: What would have happened if I allowed my past failures and challenges to dictate my decision with starting the Princess of Suburbia? I am absolutely convinced that I won't be where I am now; finally getting to do what I know I was created for.

What is your belief today? It is my hope that by now, your brain has shifted or is shifting to an arena where all things impossible have become possible for you. If it has shifted for the better, please jot down why? If not, jot down what you can do on a daily basis to adjust your thinking.

There are two acronyms I will like to leave with you, as we

wrap up this journey: **The "Stepping out FIRST" Model** as well as the **Stepping out Model itself**. These two models have helped me through the years to stay grounded and it is my hope that it will do the same for you as you digest them and genuinely apply to your life journey.

Stepping Out FIRST Model

Focus on Goals

Indulge in positive action every day

Remember goals

Seek positive yet honest feedback **(be willing to take the good and the bad- put them all to good use)**

Transfer Potential into **Next Steps**

Dr. Fumi Hancock (c) 2013

The "Stepping Out" Model

Step up and shape up!

Take charge

Exercise your potential

Perform with excellence

Overcome with your inner strength

Use your talents to achieve unlimited success

Take the initiative to succeed

Dr. Fumi Hancock (c) 2013

Fail small to succeed BIG! – Vadim Kotelnikov. We must

never be afraid of failure; because wisdom is always at the other side waiting to thrust us into success. Failure is never the problem; not learning from those mistakes and putting those mistakes to greater use is the problem. I wake up every morning thinking about these acronyms: FIRST STEP OUT! We can have the grandest ideas on the planet; we can be the greatest genius who ever lived, our success is dependent on the fact that we must **FIRST STEP OUT!** Some people live in the "potential" land for the rest of their lives; others move from that island and relocate themselves into the Next Steps land. The choice is ultimately ours to make. It is extremely important that we focus on our goals on a daily basis. It is what we put in front of us that will consume us. What are you currently obsessed about?

Nobody will always pat you in the back for a job well done. You must indulge in positive actions every day and learn to praise yourself even if you are standing alone. You will always forget a goal that is not kept in front of you; neither will you work on it. Your circle of influence is crucial to your success. Surround yourself with those who are your cheer leaders and not your dream killers. Those who will truthfully tell you when you are messing up, and praise you when needed. The goal is to ensure that you make good use of the advice you are given, good or bad. Do not be content with potentials but strive to move to the next step of your dream.

I am so very fond of the Stepping Out Model. Step up and shape up. There is no need to ramp down this your nose. In everything you do, learn to take charge. You are the master stirrer of your life… do it and do it well. Always exercise your potential for out of it will flow your destiny. In all you do, always perform in excellence as you never know who is looking. Overcome fear with your inner strength; use your talents to achieve unlimited success and take the initiative to succeed.

Just how do you begin to step out? Here is a quick snap shot of how you can begin to step into your life path. These steps are applicable in your daily work.

- Create specific goals that describe YOU.
- Take small steps toward the ultimate GOAL.
- Commit to pursuing your PLAN.
- Select activities towards your goal.
- Seek support.
- Establish time frames.
- Stretch yourself.
- Celebrate every step toward your goal

Let's quickly use today as an example of how we can simply and quickly apply these steps:

(1). Create specific goals that fit YOU:

_____

_____

_____

_____

_____

_____

_____

_____

_____

(2) What are the small steps you will make toward the
ultimate GOAL(S) starting TODAY?

_____

_____

_____

_____

_____

_____

_____

_____

_____

_____

_____

_____

_____

_____

_____

(3) What PLANS are you committed to pursuing TODAY?

----

(4) Select two or three activities towards your identified
goal(s):

----

(5). Who is in your circle of influence that can help move your goal(s) forward? If you don't have any, what plans are you going to put in place to find one? Remember a mentor can also be in the form of purchasing books featuring who we admire in our field.

----

(6) Establish time frames for these goals:

----

(7) How are you stretching yourself with these goals?

----

(8) How are you going to celebrate your success(es)? Do not go where the path may lead, g instead where there is no path and leave a trail. – Ralph Waldo Emerson.

It is time to move the mountains off your life and begin

walking in the fullness of what you were created to be. The journey begins with you:

Conceive It --- Believe It --- See It --- Receive It --- Reveal It --- Commit to It --- Implement It --- Make it known for accountability reasons.

Here is a quick recap of the "Stepping Out" Process:

Stepping Out™ Development Process

Step 1: Assess your position

Step 2: Step Out - make a conscious decision to change

Step 3: Take charge - write the vision (DREAM BIG, START SMALL to ACHIEVE BIG!)

Step 4: Develop a plan (primary & secondary)

Step 5: Create time specific goals

Step 6: Form alliances--Accountability

Step 7: Monitor your progress-Achievement plan

Step 8: Re-evaluate your goals

Step 9: Celebrate your successes

Dr. Fumi Hancock (c) 2013

THE SOLUTION: FIRST STEP-OUT

Focus on Goals

Indulge in positive action every day

Remember goals

Seek positive yet honest feedback **(be willing to take the good and the bad- put them all to good use)**

Transfer Potential into **Next Steps**

Dr. Fumi Hancock (c) 2013

Step up and shape up!

Take charge

Exercise your potential

Perform with excellence

Overcome with your inner strength

Use your talents to achieve unlimited success

Take the initiative to succeed

Believe....

Believe in yourself! Have faith in your abilities! Without a humble but reasonable confidence in your own powers you cannot be successful or happy.

Norman Vincent Peale

You are never too old to set another goal or to dream a new dream.

C.S. Lewis

Wisdom Vault....

After a storm comes a calm.
Matthew Henry

The will to win, the desire to succeed, the urge to reach your full potential… these are the keys that will unlock the door to personal excellence.
Confucius

Try to be like the turtle – at ease in your own shell.
Bill Copeland

Wisdom Vault....

- Open approach, no patent, we use green tech available;
- Solar Impulse is as wide as a Boeing, heavy as a car, has a scooter engine, and it flights!
- Its' a team of 90 people coming from all horizons who has made this dream come true in 4 years' time: in 2013, Solar Impulse achieved its first cross-America flight;
- What helped us was that we had no experience ever in building a flight!
- It is not what we do that matters, it is how we think, playing on doubts, facing the unknown to stimulate creativity, shaping a pioneer spirit - Philippe Rathle, Solar Impulse CFO.

  http://www.innovationexcellence.com/blog/2
  013/08/16/innovation-stories-
  12/#sthash.4G78Qq67.dpuf

9 CONCLUSION

It is my heartfelt desire that this book has caused your thinking to shift perhaps a little in the right direction. Knowing who we are is very significant to becoming who we desire to be. Hope is a waking dream – Aristotle. Your present circumstances do not determine where you can go; merely determine where you start – Nido Qubein. And God will always give His best to those who leave the choice with him.- Jim Elliot.

Writing this book has truly been a ride for me and I thank you for taking the time; allowing me to share some wisdom nuggets with you. It is my hope that you will continue to work in the fullness of your destiny; that this book will or has stirred up the ability and know how to move into your God ordained position; that you will daily be prompted to use the tools you have garnered therein to harness your vision and dream; that you will pass the knowledge on to others, so they too can partake of this.

I ask that you take the time to write me of your experiences with this book at: princessinsuburbia@gmail.com.

Feel free to check out updates on my mission, vision and goals… at www.worldoffumihancock.com

When all else fails, all of my social media links are posted here for your perusal:

About.me/fumihancock

I look forward to hearing your testimonials, suggestions, advice…. Afterall, we are all constantly growing, right?

Oh my the way, please be on the lookout for announcement on my upcoming movie…an original story written by me and screenplay be me. It promises to be a fun one. Information on its premiere (US & Globally)will soon be posted at: www.worldoffumihancock.com and www.ofsentimentalvalue.com.

To find out where my next conference will be: www.lesgoinnovate.com.

For updates on other books I have written and upcoming books:

www.worldoffumihancock.com

BOOKS CAN BE PURCHASED AT: **AMAZON.COM & BN.COM**

'Concentrate on what others can't achieve!'~ Gildo Pastor, Venturi Automobiles founder -
See more at:
http://www.innovationexcellence.com/blog/2013/08/16/innovation-stories-12/#sthash.4G78Qq67.dpuf

.

FOR YOUNG ADULT FANTASY LOVERS! This one's for YOU!

Amazon Bestseller!

PICK UP YOU COPY AT:

http://www.amazon.com/Fumi-Hancock/e/B009BHBI6S

Most Recent Customer Reviews on Amazon:
4.0 out of 5 stars **A Good, Good Book**
This cover is just amazing! PhatPuppy Art really did a great job with it. It's eye catching and just lovely!

The writing is good, too. The setting was just lovely.
by S. Blooding

5.0 out of 5 stars **Great YA**
The Adventures of Jewel Cardwell has the makings of a great series. In the first few pages, Jewel catches your attention and leaves you craving more.
by B. J. Gaskill

4.0 out of 5 stars **3.5 Stars Good Book - Enjoyable**
I had a bit of difficulty getting into this book initially. Jewell lives in a quiet secluded, safe neighborhood.
by L. Jenkins

4.0 out of 5 stars **This book kept me up until 4:00 a.m.!**
I wasn't sure what to expect when I started reading this book. I knew that there was some supernatural elements that would be found in the story, along with some family drama .
o by S. Staley

5.0 out of 5 stars **A Thrilling and Exciting Fantasy Adventure**
`Jewel Cardwell' is a 16 year old high school student has much to learn of her dark ancestry. As the

mysteries surrounding her family is unraveled, so does it unleash the... Read more
by Willow Mason

4.0 out of 5 stars **A new and exciting voice on the YA scene**

I have been largely dissatisfied during my occasional forays into reading YA. I started the first book in one popular series, and put it down because I felt the author was talking... Read more
Published by Andrew Kuligowski

5.0 out of 5 stars **Haunting But Well-Written**

As a parent, something about this book tugs at you. Did you do right by your children today? Have you screwed up in some way they will remember in ten years? Read more Published by Andrea Kurian

5.0 out of 5 stars **Awesome Read**

This book was very hard to put down. The plot thickens with each turn of the page. I would definitely recommend this book.
Published by Tracey Bakey

5.0 out of 5 stars **If you liked Hunger Games you will definitely like this book**

I bought this book as a present for my daughter because everyone in her class at school has read it. Read more at amazon.com

OTHER BOOKS
2RESPECTMYLIFE SERIES

HTTP://WWW.AMAZON.COM/FUMI-HANCOCK/E/B0092OE8QC

OTHER NON FICTION BOOKS

HTTP://WWW.AMAZON.COM/BEYOND-WORSHIP-STEPHANIE-OGUNLEYE-HANCOCK/DP/1602664765

HTTP://WWW.AMAZON.COM/STARTING-RIGHT-NOW-EMPOWERMENT-SELF-FULFILLMENT/DP/0595205275/

ABOUT THE AUTHOR
THE PRINCESS OF SUBURBIA™
PRINCESS FUMI S HANCOCK, M.A,PH.D.

©Copyright 2013 Princess Fumi Hancock

While living in New York she hosted, produced and directed a local show Christian "Straight Talk" in conjunction with the Rhema Prayer Ministries, Inc. as well as a 30 minutes talk show called "Stepping Out with Dr Fumi." In addition, she has coordinated several programs for women and children with many social service agencies in New York and New Jersey areas, ranging from foster care, adoption, second chance homes for battered women.

As the President of Adassa Adumori Foundation, a US based 501(c)3 nonprofit organization in Tennessee, doing work in Africa and other 3rd World countries; she recently interviewed the African Union Ambassador to the US. She is a noted Mental Health columnist for the New American Times, an Immigrant Newspaper serving Middle Tennessee and has been invited to guest speak at several women's conferences in the US as well as address governmental leaders such as governors and highly placed business executives in the international arena.

Fumi has been featured in various newspapers and online magazines such as Princeton Packet, The Tennessean. She has been instrumental in assisting start-up organization with their business development and is often called on to help dysfunctional organizations get back to the successful road. She has also written several inspirational Books, Starting Right Now, Diary of an African Princess as well as eBooks: **2Respectmylife.com**; Her Online Television Program: **Princess in Suburbia** was recently released in the year (2013). It is a place dedicated to love, life, relationships and everything in-between. With many women (men alike requesting to be coached by dynamic Innovation Gurus) alongside Yolanda Shields, they are preparing to launch their very first Business Coaching Enterprise **Let's Go Innovate**™ with a city tour across the United States of America.

Fumi "Stephanie" Hancock is a walking example of how an ordinary person from a shackled life of broken promises and shattered dreams can live a fulfilled destiny. After twenty years of dropping her pen, she picks it right back up again by releasing November 2012 Teens Amazon Bestseller -The Grimmlyn Series: **The Adventures of Jewell Cardwell,** Hydra's Nest. Though graduated with a postgraduate degree in communication arts, and undergraduate degrees in English studies and nursing, she ascribes her writing to her life experiences. She aspires to one day write a mystery/detective novel for the adult audience. But for now, she is content with her young adult audience. With her background in nursing, she gently nurses her unusual characters to life for her readers to enjoy. Her second book in the Grimmlyn series, **The Sorcerer's Purgatory** is scheduled for release soon.

Writing to help people find their path to destiny is yet another arena she is soaring under let leadership as the President of Let's Go Innovate.

Be on the lookout for her very **first feature film** as the executive producer and the screenwriter…
www.worldoffumihancock.com

On the Air with Princess in Suburbia: The PREMIERE ON BLOGTALKRADIO

The Princess in Suburbia TV

Made in the USA
Charleston, SC
16 October 2013